Population, Resources and the Environment

The Critical Challenges

UNFPA

United Nations
Population Fund

ACKNOWLEDGEMENTS

This study was researched and drafted by Norman Myers, and was subsequently revised taking into account comments and suggestions from several individuals. We would like to acknowledge, in particular, the contributions of David Horlacher, Aprodicio Laquian, Alex Marshall, Stafford Mousky, Lamine N'Diaye, Jeannie Peterson, Catherine Pierce, Raheem Sheikh, Mari Simonen, Jyoti Singh, Kerstin Trone, and Ugur Tuncer. In addition, Don Hinrichsen prepared the revised text for publication, and Paul Shaw served as the general editor for this project. The views expressed herein are not necessarily those of UNFPA or any of the member states.

ISBN 0-89714-101-6

Typesetting by Typecast Graphics
Cover design by Roger Whisker
Cover picture by R. Giling/Panos
Printed in USA by Automated Graphic Systems

A **Banson** production
3 Turville Street
London E2 7HR, UK

FOREWORD

In 1987, the World Commission on Environment and Development challenged the international community and national governments to work towards a sustainable future: a pattern of development that broadens the choices for future generations.

At its 1987 session, the United Nations General Assembly called for "a balance between population and environment capacities as would make possible sustainable development, keeping in view the links among population levels, consumption patterns, poverty and the natural resource base."

In December 1990, the General Assembly once again emphasized the importance of "addressing the relationship between demographic pressures and unsustainable consumption patterns and environmental degradation during the preparatory process of the United Nations Conference on Environment and Development..."

As we enter the Fourth United Nations Development Decade, our common purpose is to narrow the economic gap between people in the developed and developing worlds. The task before the international community, and each country, is to re-examine the population-resource balance; to correct inefficient and wasteful use of resources; and to seek for optimal population growth and distribution patterns in an integrated, comprehensive move towards sustainability.

Two development issues stand out. First, despite much effort, no solution has been found for the deepening *poverty* of individuals and nations. Globally, more than a billion people are living in absolute poverty, and the total international debt of low-income countries is more than $1,000 billion and climbing. Second, the *social sector* – including health, family planning, housing and education – continues to be underemphasized in national and international development programmes. At the national level, developing countries have struggled to keep pace with the needs of populations which have often doubled in the last 30 years. Yet, demands for health care, education, food security, housing and jobs are still increasing, and will continue to increase through the next decade.

It is unrealistic to discuss sustainable development and a common future without reference to the environment and the world's resource base. The debate is also meaningless if population is ushered to the sidelines. Population issues are central to the search for sustainability. World population now stands at almost 5.4 billion, and it will increase during this decade at an average of over 95 million people every year.

By the year 2001, the total will reach 6.4 billion. Ninety-six per cent of population growth is in developing countries, with the fastest growth found in the poorest areas. Moreover, half the population of developing countries is under 25; urban growth rates are almost three times those of more developed countries and international migration from South to North is rising steadily.

Of course, population, resource and environmental issues are linked in complex ways and at different levels of development. For example, much of the environmental degradation witnessed today is due primarily to two groups of people – the top billion richest and the bottom billion poorest. The top consumers in North America, Europe and Asia destroy the environment more indirectly through their frightening ability to consume resources and generate vast quantities of waste. The bottom billion poorest destroy their own resource base out of necessity and lack of options. But, in both cases, population is an issue.

The main focus of this book is on the intricate, sometimes complicated, inter-relationships between population, resources and the environment. It is an attempt to deal with these complex issues in a comprehensive manner, offering many detailed examples to bolster the central thesis.

Dr. Nafis Sadik
Executive Director
United Nations Population Fund (UNFPA), October 1991

CONTENTS

The Critical Challenges

"The 'triad' of excessive population growth, environmental degradation and poverty threaten us and our planet as never before."

Declaration of the International Forum on Population in the Twenty-First Century, Amsterdam, 6-9 November, 1989.

"We all agree that a national population policy is a necessity... and that the rate of population growth should not be such as to impose unduly severe pressure on the environment. To ignore these strictures is to court disaster, as recent experience has amply demonstrated around the world."

Robert Mugabe, Prime Minister of Zimbabwe, at the International Forum on Population in the Twenty-First Century, Amsterdam, 6-9 November, 1989.

"Population pressure, pushing farmers onto increasingly marginal land, is a major cause of ecological problems in many countries, particularly the poorer ones. Curbing population growth is essential for sustainable economic growth."

Barber Conable, President of the World Bank, 1987.

"If we do not get population growth under control, habitat on Earth will be destroyed by ecological disaster and/or violent migration processes."

Willy Brandt, former Chancellor of West Germany, at the International Forum on Population in the Twenty-First Century, Amsterdam, 6-9 November, 1989.

EXECUTIVE SUMMARY

The pressures generated by population growth reflect two key demographic factors: the rate of population growth, and the absolute numbers of additional people added to the global total each year. While the first has been declining for the last several decades (apart from a slight recent upsurge), the second will continue to increase for some time into the future. During the 1990s there will be an annual increment of almost 100 million people, the highest ever.

This unprecedented rapid growth in human numbers, plus their distributional patterns and urbanization trends, induces critical constraints on the development process, as well as unsustainable burdens on the environmental resource base that underpins much economic activity in developing countries. In addition, it overwhelms the planning capacities of governments to cater for fast-growing communities. There is generally not enough time to supply the socio-economic infrastructure, notably in the form of basic services and amenities, to accommodate increasing numbers of people.

Population growth is particularly significant for the poorest of the poor, the "bottom billion" who cause environmental degradation in their pursuit of survival and who cannot afford to engage in resource-conserving measures. These people feature the highest population growth rates, and have least access to information, education and services in maternal and child health care and family planning.

The most disadvantaged of all developing-world people tend to be women. Their social status should be thoroughly enhanced as a matter of basic equity. At the same time, women offer much potential as "environmental managers", in addition to their obviously vital part in population programmes. Both environmental and population causes can be markedly advanced through efforts to upgrade the overall status of women.

Much environmental degradation stems from developed nations too, notably in the form of atmospheric pollution and global warming with their worldwide impacts. While this is primarily a problem of inappropriate technologies and excessive consumerism, it also reflects the population growth factor.

The adverse environmental impacts of population growth, high fertility levels, uneven distribution and other factors, particularly in developing countries, derive from a range of factors, both direct and indirect, both overt and covert, working through linkages that are both proximate and ultimate. Among the complex mix of variables in

3

question are deficient development strategies and such exogenous factors as international debt and inequitable trade-and-aid relations between developing and developed countries.

There has been much theoretical debate about the purported linkages between population growth and environmental degradation. Yet the linkages involved have received all too little attention in the way of rigorous analysis and detailed documentation. Nor have they been adequately addressed through policy initiatives and programme measures. It is the aim of this study to identify, define, clarify and evaluate the linkages in question. In doing so, the study provides a comprehensive review of the impact of population on natural resources and the environment so as to communicate the issues involved, the prospects for remedying population impacts through incisive interventions and the kinds of policies needed to bring about more comprehensive solutions.

In sum, population factors are among the many forces that serve to undermine the environmental resource base upon which sustainable development ultimately depends. In many countries there is a pronounced imbalance between the growth and distribution of population on the one hand and the natural resource endowment on the other hand – albeit with much differentiated impact according to countries and development sectors. Hence, there is a premium on slowing population growth with all due dispatch as a pre-eminent measure to safeguard the global environment.

In response to these population and environment challenges, there is extensive scope for policy interventions, plus action-oriented programmes to remedy imbalances in population growth and distribution. Policy measures undertaken during the 1990s will go far to shape the world for much of the next century. There is a premium on urgent and vigorous action, if only because the resource scarcest in supply is time itself.

CHAPTER 1

INTRODUCTION

As the 20th century draws to a close, the world is confronted by a daunting challenge: to bring growing human numbers and their growing needs into balance with the natural resource base that underpins much development. Choices made during the next 10 years will determine, to a large extent, the future habitability of the planet. The collision between human numbers and the resources needed to sustain them will become more acute in the remaining years of this century and beyond.[1-3]

A good part of the struggle to balance population with available natural resources will be concentrated in the developing world where human numbers, in many instances, have already exceeded the "red line" of resource use. As pressures intensify, some experts even envision the outbreak of resource wars in the developing world with worldwide repercussions.[4]

The environmental dimension to population is firmly grounded in economics, among other factors. Behind the demographic issues of population growth and its uneven distribution, fertility levels, age-dependency ratios, migration patterns and urbanization, lies the imperative of economic advancement and sustainable development. The attempt to arrive at a new economic order, an order that promotes the sustainable use of natural resources at environmentally acceptable rates, is the key to long-term development.

The search for sustainability must be addressed within the context of population and natural resource issues. It is widely recognized that the current economic order does not promote sustainable development. Quite the contrary; we are using up the Earth's store of natural resources at demonstrably non-sustainable rates and triggering extensive damage to the biosphere. Environmental degradation on such a massive scale cannot continue indefinitely. It is essential that governments, aid agencies, international institutions and non-governmental organizations (NGOs) advance the concept of sustainable management of the Earth's stock of natural resources, so that current generations will be able to broaden – not narrow – the choices future generations will have available. We can no longer afford to borrow from the future to pay for the present.

When the linkages between population growth, its distribution and environmental degradation enter the economic equation, the development outlook is altered profoundly. It is becoming apparent that we have achieved economic advancement in the past at a major cost to the future's capacity to supply still more economic development – and even at the more serious cost of an actual decline in human welfare. Much of what has passed for economic achievement may prove illusory in the long run. Many of our technological innovations have contributed to environmental decline and are turning out to be no more than temporary "fixes", merely deferring the day when the accumulated though hidden costs will have to be paid in full.

Consider the case of Green Revolution agriculture which enabled growth in grain production to keep ahead of growth in human numbers throughout the period 1950 to 1984. There appear to have been many covert costs attached to this agricultural advancement. The continued overloading of cropland soils – brought on by over-dosing of fertilizers and pesticides and intensive cropping – has led to broad-scale erosion, depletion of soil nutrients and salinization and waterlogging, among other environmental injuries. Salinization and waterlogging result from irrigation projects that have not taken account of the need for proper drainage: salts accumulate in the soil, effectively sterilizing it, and the water table rises until it chokes off the crop roots.

These deleterious practices, while unnoticed or disregarded for decades, are now levying a price in terms of falling agricultural productivity. Take India and Pakistan as examples. In India, 200,000 square kilometres – 36 per cent of irrigated lands – are so salinized that they have lost much of their productivity, while Pakistan has lost 32,000 square kilometres – 20 per cent – to salinization. Yet these two countries have often been ranked among the prime exponents of Green Revolution agriculture. The world total of salinized lands is estimated at 600,000 square kilometres or 22 per cent of all irrigated lands.[5]

Environmental constraints of several sorts are now causing significant cutbacks in food production at a time when population growth continues with scant restraint. Soil erosion leads to an annual loss in grain output that is roughly estimated at 9 million tonnes. Salinization and waterlogging of irrigated lands account for another million tonnes; and a combination of loss of soil organic matter (through burning of livestock manure and crop residues for fuel), shortening of shifting-cultivator cycles, and soil compaction, for 2 million tonnes. In all, these forms of land degradation reduce grain harvests by some 12 million tonnes a year. On top of this are various types of other damage to crop production: air pollution reduces grain production by a million tonnes each year. Flooding, acid rain and increased ultraviolet radiation account for another million tonnes in lost production.

The total loss from all forms of environmental degradation adds up to an estimated 14 million tonnes of grain output a year. This total is to be compared with gains from increased irrigation, fertilizer use and other inputs, worth 29 million tonnes a year. In other words, environmental factors are now causing the loss of almost half of all gains from technology-based advances in agriculture. It is a loss we can ill afford, since the world needs an additional 28 million tonnes of grain output each year just to feed additional numbers of people at current nutritional levels. While the net gain in grain output amounts to less than 1 per cent each year, the world population is growing almost twice as fast, at 1.7 per cent.[5]

In other sectors too, the hidden costs of many activities associated with economic development have taken their toll on the environment. Before reunification of the two Germanys, the non-sustainable use of natural resources, coupled with environmental degradation from economic development, was costing West Germany some 20 billion marks a year, a full 10 per cent of the country's Gross National Product (GNP).[6] Such costs call into question the very concept of economic growth as conventionally understood, given its progressive depletion of a given country's stock of resources. It also highlights flaws in national accounting systems which calculate economic advancement in an "environmental vacuum".

Developing countries pay an even higher price for neglecting environmental accounting. According to Dr. Robert Repetto, an economist with the World Resources Institute in Washington, DC, "Ironically, low-income countries, which are typically most dependent on natural resources for employment, revenues, and foreign-exchange earnings are instructed to use a system for national accounting that almost completely ignores their principal assets. A country could exhaust its mineral resources, cut down its forests, erode its soils, pollute its aquifers, and hunt its wildlife and fisheries to extinction, but measured income would not be affected as these assets disappeared."[7]

While searching for a future that incorporates the key factor of sustainable development, the international community will have to devise new ways of measuring economic growth in order to incorporate both environmental and population factors.

As an intrinsic part of this process, the vast economic gap between developed and developing countries must be narrowed. Two areas in particular need to be addressed: restructuring of the debt burden and more equitable trade arrangements. Developing countries now owe around $1.3 trillion to developed-country banks and lending institutions. This debt burden weighs heavily on developing-world prospects for development generally, and on population and environment concerns in particular. In sub-Saharan Africa, for example, public long-term debt amounted to 58 per cent of the region's GNP in 1986, climbing to over 90 per cent by 1990.[8] The debt crisis has prompted many poor countries to cut back on government spending for health care and family planning activities, thus contributing to a slow-down in fertility rate declines in the Philippines, India, Tunisia, Morocco, Colombia and Costa Rica.[1]

The gross imbalance in international trade also contributes to the non-sustainable use of resources and, indirectly, to excessive migration and urbanization among other things. To shield themselves against cheaper food imports from the developing world, the industrialized countries of North America and Western Europe spend $200 billion a year in agricultural subsidies to protect domestic markets.[9] These subsidies militate against agricultural exports from developing countries, depriving them of trade revenues worth about $30 billion a year.[10,11] In turn, these direct losses reduce developing-world farmers' profits, leaving them less to invest in better seeds, fertilizers and equipment. In addition, many developing-country farmers often receive little government incentive to stay on their farmsteads – in many instances crop prices are artificially low – and many of them over-cultivate their small plots or are forced to open up marginal areas in an effort to scratch a living from the land. Where there is a fixed amount of agricultural land and rapidly increasing populations to be supported on them, farm plots are often split into smaller and smaller fragments until they can no longer support a household. Millions of farmers have been driven off their lands and into cities where they swell shanty towns and slums, contributing to the crisis in urban services and furthering environmental degradation.[12]

The imperatives of sustainable development are equally significant for the developed world. The level of a country's economic development and its consumption patterns make a crucial difference as concerns natural resource use. Take energy as an example. Whereas each Bangladeshi consumes commercial energy equivalent to only 3 barrels of oil a year, each American consumes 55 barrels, implying that the population-derived increase in Bangladesh's consumption of oil in 1990 is equivalent to only 8.7 million barrels, that of the United

States 110 million barrels.

The developed-world countries with their highly advanced infrastructure are in a much better position to conserve natural resources and produce less waste and pollution than developing countries saddled with vast numbers of people living on the edge of survival. Enhanced management of natural resources, for instance through energy-efficiency and conservation plans, would not only make economic sense for developed countries, but could also produce spinoff benefits for developing countries, taking the form of energy supplies at cheaper prices and the transfer of environmentally-sound technologies.

There are multiple sets of dynamic interactions involved between population growth and environmental deterioration. Both are central to the cause of sustainable development. So strategies to promote sustainable development must integrate population and environmental concerns alike. Without such policy integration, sustainable development will remain nothing more than a proclamation on paper.

THE POPULATION DIMENSION

In mid-1990, the world contained 5.3 billion people. Of these, 4.1 billion, or 77 per cent of the total, lived in developing countries, and 1.2 billion, or 23 per cent, in developed countries. The global total was growing at a rate of 1.7 per cent a year, with an average of 79 million people a year during the 1980s. This means that during 1990 the world's population expanded by the equivalent of another Mexico.

WORLD POPULATION GROWTH BY DECADE, 1950-1990
WITH PROJECTIONS TO 2000

Year	Population (billions)	Average increase each decade (millions)	Average increase each year (millions)
1950	2.516	n/a	n/a
1960	3.040	524	52
1970	3.698	658	66
1980	4.448	750	75
1990	5.292	844	84
2000	6.260	968	97

WORLD POPULATION GROWTH BY REGIONS

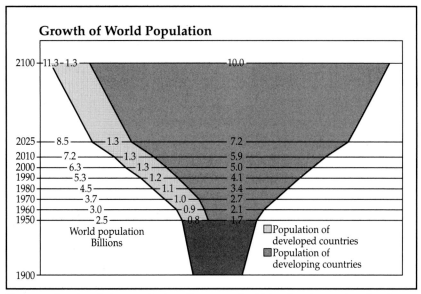

Growth of World Population

Figures are based on the latest projections. These are rather higher than those projected until recently, due to a slowing down in the decline of fertility rates in a number of countries.

Population by region, in billions

Region	1990	2025	2100	Region	1990	2025	2100
Africa	0.6	1.6	3.0	North America	0.3	0.3	0.3
Asia	3.1	4.9	6.3	Europe & USSR	0.8	0.9	0.8
Latin America & Caribbean	0.5	0.8	0.9	Oceania	0.03*	0.04	0.04

Annual growth rate as measured in 1990 and time for the population to double

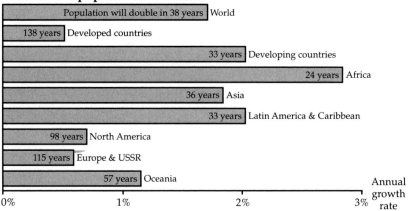

Population will double in 38 years | World
138 years | Developed countries
33 years | Developing countries
24 years | Africa
36 years | Asia
33 years | Latin America & Caribbean
98 years | North America
115 years | Europe & USSR
57 years | Oceania

Annual growth rate

0%   1%   2%   3%

Of this annual increase, more than 90 per cent is in developing countries. These countries tend to be least able to cope with the development and environmental consequences of rapid growth in human numbers due to their low per capita incomes, indebtedness, and limited capacity for investments.[1,13,14,15]

The latest projections[16,17,18] indicate that the global total will reach 6.3 billion people by the year 2000 and 8.5 billion by 2025, before levelling out at an eventual total of 11.3 billion by the end of next century or shortly thereafter. These figures are rather higher than those projected a few years ago (6.1 billion, 8.2 billion and 10.2 billion), due to a slowing down in the decline of fertility rates in a number of countries. This is notably the case in China and India which together account for more than half of the upward revisions. Other such countries include the Philippines, Malawi, Tunisia, Morocco, Colombia and Costa Rica. Of the projected increase of 3.2 billion from 1990 until 2025 – at least 3 billion, or 94 per cent, will occur in developing countries which, because of the challenges they already face, are least able to accommodate population growth on this scale within such a short time frame.

Moreover, the 11.3 billion figure for the eventual world total is the medium-level projection. The high projection indicates the total could reach 14.2 billion by the year 2100, while the low projection reveals that global population could be held to just under 8 billion. The difference between the high and low projections is substantial, 6.3 billion people: more than the entire world population by the turn of the century.

This represents an unprecedented rate of rapid population growth. The increase in the last 40 years equals the total increase during the half million years from the emergence of *Homo sapiens* until 1950. It is not only a very recent phenomenon; it can be no more than a very transitory phenomenon. For 99.9 per cent of humankind's existence, the maximum world population was less than 10 million people, or fewer than now live in several large cities. Population growth was only about 0.001 per cent a year, by contrast with today's rate of 1.8 per cent a year, 1,800 times greater. The first billion mark was not reached until around 1830. It took another 100 years or so, until 1930, before the world's population increased to 2 billion. The third billion was added by 1960 (30 years), a fourth by 1974 (14 years), and a fifth by 1987 (13 years). The 6-billionth inhabitant of Earth will probably be born sometime during 1998 (11 years), and the 7-billionth by around 2009 (11 years). The last 3 billion (supposing an eventual total of rather more than 11 billion) will be added by 2100 or so (91 years), the bulk of them by 2050.[16] Such a massive increase in human numbers, occurring virtually instantaneously in a historical perspective, is proving to be highly disruptive in terms of our capacities to plan for and to support ever faster growing numbers.

So while the global rate of population growth has declined a good deal – from a high of 2.1 per cent in the late 1960s to 1.7 per cent today – the number of people added to the total each year, now 84 million, is higher than ever before. Moreover, it is projected to keep on climbing for a while to come, reaching an annual peak of 97 million by the year 2000. As we shall see, it is the annual increase in absolute numbers that is so critical to countries' prospects for sustainable development, meaning, in the broadest sense, development based on safeguarding the world's environmental resource base. Alternatively stated, the incremental increase in human numbers is more important than the rate of population growth – closely related though the two factors obviously are.

Note, however, that these demographic projections are extrapolations of recent trends, together with some assumptions about the role of economic advancement and family planning in stemming the rate of population growth. Projections are not predictions, still less are they forecasts. By their nature they take no account of other variables such as policy changes and technological breakthroughs.[19,20,21] Nor do they reflect environmental factors: they assume there will be no Malthusian constraints. But the fast-growing degradation of the natural resource base that ultimately supports all communities may soon start – in the absence of incisively remedial measures – to exert a constraining effect on population growth. Given the record of the last two decades, it becomes increasingly hard to see how sub-Saharan Africa, for example, will experience a projected quadrupling of human numbers within another century as long as gross environmental impoverishment continues to spread in the manner of the recent past. Those who consider that population growth may soon be pressing against or even exceed "population carrying capacity" (an important concept introduced at the start of Chapter 3) are inclined to be increasingly sceptical about demographic projections made in an "environmental vacuum".

Within this overall perspective a number of demographic trends reflect a disturbing reality: one which will have profound repercussions. In terms of birth and death rates, developing countries can be divided roughly into three groups, each of which manifests demographic momentum of alarming proportions:[15]

- Thirty-two per cent, or 1.3 billion, of the people in the developing world live in countries such as China and the Republic of Korea, where birth rates are below 25, death rates below 10 and infant mortality is below 50 (per 1,000 population in all cases); population growth rates are now 1 to 1.14 per cent a year, enough to produce an annual increase of roughly 15 million people each year.

• Forty-one per cent, or 1.72 billion, are in countries such as Brazil, parts of India, Indonesia and Mexico, where birth rates have fallen (but not as much as death rates), where infant mortality is moderate (between 50 and 75) and population is still growing at around 2 per cent each year, sufficient to double it every 35 years.

• The remaining 27 per cent, or 1.1 billion, live in regions such as sub-Saharan Africa, parts of the Middle East and much of South Asia, where death rates have fallen, but birth rates (over 30) and infant mortality (over 100) remain high. Their populations are doubling every 23 to 28 years.

Furthermore, the youthful age structure accompanying rapid population growth means that a large proportion of the current population is supported by those people of economically productive ages. In the developing world, there are 2.3 people of working age to support each school-age child, compared to 4.1 in the developed world.

Some 36 per cent of people living in developing countries are under 15 years of age. Their fertility as adults will make an enormous difference to population growth rates next century, and consequently to the global environment. With an early start on child bearing, teenage mothers often end up having large families. If their daughters also marry early, the pattern repeats itself, and the gap between generations is shortened, fuelling the momentum of population growth. The United Nations medium projection for population growth, cited earlier, assumes that world fertility will be at replacement level by 2035; a 30-year delay would mean an extra 4 billion people.[15]

Because of the youthfulness of developing-world populations, these countries will have an enormous task in creating employment opportunities. The labour force in developing countries is projected to grow from around 1.7 billion today to more than 3.1 billion by the year 2025. Every year another 38 million new jobs will be needed, not counting jobs required to wipe out existing unemployment and underemployment (estimated at 40 per cent of the work force in many developing countries). This burden will create tremendous economic, social and political pressures, leading to increased poverty, mass migrations, civil unrest and further depletion of the natural resource base.[1]

An additional concern is the growing numbers of elderly in both the developed and developing worlds. Life expectancy averages 70 to 76 years in industrialized countries, and is now 60 to 65 years in many developing countries. Although this represents a success in health terms, it has many economic and social implications, not only for dependency ratios, but for the future of the family unit. The spectre of large numbers of young people, with growing cohorts of elderly, will put increased strain on developing-world governments least able to afford them.

POPULATION AGE PYRAMIDS 1985 & 2025

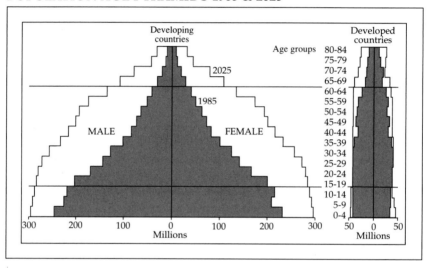

A further dimension to this demographic background impinges on environmental questions. It is the distribution of population, and especially the massive shift from rural to urban areas, a process that is largely confined to developing countries. In 1985, the world's urban population was just over 2.1 billion people. It is projected to climb to 3.2 billion by 2000, and to soar to 5.5 billion by 2025. This means it could well multiply by a factor of 2.6 during the period 1985-2000, and by a factor of 1.7 during the period 2000-2025 – or rates that are 2.0 and 4.0 per cent higher than rates for population growth overall. In the developing world, the urban population is projected to increase from 1.5 billion to 3.5 billion, a 133 per cent expansion during just the next 15 years. As early as 2010, the developing world's rural population is projected to reach 2.8 billion people. Thereafter it is expected to stop growing altogether, possibly even going into decline.[16] So one of the most dominant trends in the developing world is ultra-rapid if not excessive urbanization.

Rapid urbanization – stemming in major measure from population growth – has many implications for environmental conditions in developing-world cities. The pressure of fast-growing human numbers engenders acute shortages of many basic requirements for acceptable living standards, including supplies of water, sanitation, food, energy, housing and sheer space. Huge congregations of urban communities (well over half the total population in many instances) are obliged to exist in shanty towns and slums, amidst extreme squalor and deprivation. Moreover, urban concentrations of impoverished people tend to exert a parasitic impact on their resource support zones in the hinterlands, contributing, for example, to accelerating deforestation through unsustainable demand for fuelwood.

The outlook for more than a billion absolutely impoverished people in developing countries is bleak. These "poorest of the poor", being most in need of the benefits of development, are often responsible for a disproportionate amount of environmental degradation, and feature the highest fertility rates.[22] They totalled less than 0.5 billion in 1975, or 23 per cent of developing-world populations, but their number has now risen to 1.2 billion, still 23 per cent (see diagram on the next page). While their percentage share of total numbers is likely to decline, their absolute numbers are projected to keep on increasing (in the absence of vigorous remedial measures) until well into the next century.

Populations of the developed countries of North America, Europe, and Asia and the Pacific also bear a large responsibility for environmental degradation at the global level. Their population growth of 0.8 per cent or less a year is allied with an exceptional technological and consumerist capacity to exploit natural resources and generate enormous quantities of waste. These developed countries consume a disproportionate share of the Earth's natural resources. With barely 25 per cent of the planet's population, they account for 75 per cent of all energy used, 79 per cent of all commercial fuels and 85 per cent of all wood products. Even more important, they generate nearly three quarters of all carbon dioxide emissions that account for half of global warming, plus a similarly disproportionate share of other greenhouse gases.

PEOPLE ESTIMATED TO BE LIVING IN ABSOLUTE POVERTY, 1989

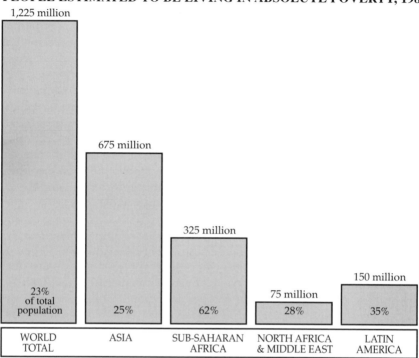

CRITICAL LINKAGES

There are several sets of linkages at work between population and environment. What are their scope and scale? How do they operate? Do they act in both directions? What variations occur among countries and cultures? What are some time horizons in question? Since the question of linkages is central to this analysis, let us examine them in some detail.

Consider, first, the central factors of population growth and its impacts. We can identify four principal components: P, being population itself, I, being environmental impact, A, being per capita consumption (determined by income and lifestyle), and T, being environmentally harmful technology that supplies A.[23] The three factors P, A and T interact in multiplicative fashion; in other words, they compound each other's impacts. So whatever the size of A and T, the role of P is bound to be significant even when a population and its growth rate are relatively small. For any type of technology, for any given level of consumption or waste, for any given level of poverty or inequality, the more people there are, the greater is their overall impact on the environment.[23] So we can represent the processes involved in the form of a basic equation, I = PAT.[23]

This basic equation demonstrates why developing nations, with large populations but limited economic advancement, can generate a vast impact on the environment (hence on prospects for sustainable development), if only because the P multiplier on the A and T factors is so large. Likewise, the equation makes clear that developed nations also generate population impacts insofar as the A and T multipliers for each person are exceptionally large.

At the same time, a number of other factors are at work in addition to the three elements of the equation. They include socio-economic inequities, cultural constraints, government policies and the international economic order. Moreover, these additional factors vary greatly throughout the global community of almost 200 nations, disparate as they are in agro-climatic zones, natural resource endowments and historical traditions. But sooner or later all these additional factors operate through one or another of the equation's three variables. (Another way to look at the interconnections between demographic and

THE LINKAGES BETWEEN DEMOGRAPHIC AND NATURAL RESOURCE ISSUES

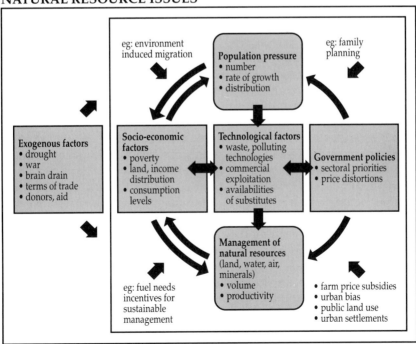

natural resource factors is set out in the diagram on the previous page).

To illustrate how the equation's interactions work, suppose that, by dint of exceptional effort, humankind managed to reduce the average per capita consumption of environmental resources (A in the equation) by 5 per cent; and to improve its technologies (T) so that they cause an average of 5 per cent less environmental injury. This would reduce the total impact (I) of humanity by roughly 10 per cent. But unless the rate of global population growth (P) – now 1.7 per cent a year – were restrained at the same time, it would bring the total impact back to the previous level within less than 6 years.

Variants of the basic equation yield insights into the role of population growth on the part of a particular sector of humankind, the billion people who live in absolute poverty. In this case, environmental impact (I) is related to population, poverty, and the environmental resources available to support the impoverished multitudes. The interactions are again multiplicative, each one reinforcing the others' impacts. But in this case, the communities in question tend to feature the highest population growth rates. Of the poorest fifth of developing-world households, between 55 and 80 per cent have eight or more members, whereas among all households at national level the proportion is only 15 to 30 per cent.[26] Moreover, these people are unusually dependent for their survival upon the environmental resource base of soil, water, forests, fisheries and biotas that make up their main stocks of economic capital. Regrettably, they often see scant alternative to exploiting their environmental resource base at a rate they recognize is surely unsustainable. They thereby undercut their principal means of livelihood, thus entrenching their poverty. In turn, this appears to reinforce their motivation to have large families.[27] As a result, they face the prospect of ever tightening constraints.

Their plight also reflects the failure of development in general. They have been bypassed by the usual forms of development, notably Green Revolution agriculture, and they cannot afford costly inputs such as high-yielding seeds, fertilizer, irrigation and farm machinery. So these people become "marginalized". They are marginalized, too, in that they generally lack economic, political, legal or social status, meaning they can do little to remedy their plight. All too often this drives them to seek livelihoods in environments that are unsuitable for sustainable agriculture, being too wet, too dry or too steep. Hence, there is the phenomenon of the impoverished peasant who causes deforestation, desertification and soil erosion on a wide scale: a case of the marginal person in marginal environments. In developing countries as a whole, these "bottom billion" people may often impose greater environmental injury than the other 3 billion of their fellow citizens put together.

In short, far from enjoying the development benefits that would ostensibly push them through a demographic transition to smaller families, these people are caught in a demographic trap. Given their severely constrained circumstances, population growth denies them the very inducements that could serve to reduce population growth.[27]

A third variation of the conceptual framework deals with population pressures reflected through urbanization. The mass migration of rural people to cities of the developing world is one of the more prominent processes of the late 20th century. The situation can be represented by I = PMR, where I is again the impact (still more localized this time, though not confined to the cities themselves), P is population growth, M is the rate of migration, and R is the natural resource stock that sustains urban communities. The last part of this equation refers not only to resources within the cities – land, water and the like – but to resources in the hinterland zones that support urban populations, such as food and fuel.

This last example points up a further factor that applies to all three sets of linkages. Governments have the capacity to manage the processes involved (population growth, increased consumerism and technology expansion), provided they explicitly plan for them. But this would require a host of government activities: political responses, policy interventions, institutional initiatives, promotion of technological advances, and measures to expand socio-economic infrastructure.

All of this makes for a planning challenge unprecedented in its character and extent. No societies in the past have had to cater for population growth at annual rates of 2 per cent or more for decades on end, let alone the rates of 3 to 4 per cent that have recently characterized a sizable number of nations in sub-Saharan Africa and the Arab world. Indeed, it would tax the planning capacities of the most sophisticated and established societies. Yet, it is a challenge confronting nations that often have experienced only a few decades of nationhood and the modern state system. Moreover, many developing nations are further constrained by exogenous factors such as adverse trade relations, inadequate and often inequitable aid flows and foreign debt. In these circumstances, it is remarkable that so many developing nations have managed to achieve so much in so short a period.

Ecological dislocations

Thus, we see that growth in human numbers, in conjunction with growth in human consumption and growth in environmentally adverse technology (the I = PAT equation), can combine to precipitate a downturn in the capacity of environmental resources to sustain human communities at their current consumption levels. In certain instances, this produces ecological discontinuities or threshold effects of irreversible injury. These occur when ecosystems have absorbed stresses over long periods without much outward sign of damage, then suddenly reach a disruption level at which the cumulative consequences of stress finally reveal themselves in critical proportions. One such example is the widespread dieback of conifers in upland areas of Europe and eastern North America. We can well anticipate that as human communities continue to expand in numbers, they will exert increasing pressures on ecosystems and natural resource stocks, whereupon ecological discontinuities will surely become more common.

The Philippines provide a good example. Following the closing of the agricultural frontier in the lowlands during the 1970s, multitudes of landless people started to migrate into the uplands, leading to a buildup of human numbers at a rate far greater than that of the national population growth. The uplands contain the bulk of the country's remaining tropical forests. The result has been a marked increase in deforestation and soil erosion. In other words, there has occurred a "breakpoint" in patterns of human settlement and environmental degradation. As long as the lowlands were less than fully occupied, it made little difference to the uplands whether there was 50 per cent or 10 per cent space left. It was only when hardly any space at all was left that the situation deteriorated radically. What had seemed acceptable became critical and a profound shift occurred in a very short space of time.[28]

The problem of land shortages, accompanied by farmland fragmentation, is becoming widespread in many if not most developing countries, where land provides the main livelihood for almost 60 per cent of their populations and where most of the fertile and accessible land has already been occupied. During the 1970s, arable areas were expanding at roughly 0.5 per cent a year. But during the 1980s, the rate dropped to only half as much. And primarily because of population growth, the amount of per capita arable land declined by 1.9 per cent a year.[1] As far back as 1975, some 25 million square kilometres of land were worked by 1.2 billion people, yet only 563 million of them could be fed sustainably with the low-technology farming methods generally practised. Many of these lands were in semi-arid or montane zones, susceptible to soil erosion. Population overloading served to aggravate the pace of land degradation.[29]

Consider too an instance where a potentially renewable resource suddenly becomes overwhelmed by rapid population growth. Most people in the developing world derive their energy from fuelwood. As long as the number of wood collectors does not exceed the capacity of the tree stock to replenish itself through regrowth, the local community can exploit the resource indefinitely. They may keep on increasing in numbers for decades, indeed centuries, and all is well, provided they do not surpass a critical level of exploitation. But what if the number of collectors grows until they finally exceed the self-renewing capacity of the trees – perhaps exceeding it by only a small amount? Quite suddenly a point is reached where forest cover starts to decline. Season by season the self-renewing capacity becomes ever more depleted: the exploitation load remains the same, and so the resource keeps on dwindling. More and more, a vicious circle is set up, and it proceeds to tighten once the level of exploitation becomes non-linear.

Note that this scenario applies even if the number of collectors stops growing. The damage is done. But if the number of collectors continues to expand through population growth or migration, the double degree of overloading (derived from an ever shrinking stock exploited by ever more collectors) becomes compounded. There ensues a positive feedback process that leads to acute fuelwood scarcity, and then all too quickly the stock is depleted to zero. The process occurs all the more rapidly as the stock is progressively used up.

The essence of the situation is that the pace of critical change can be rapid indeed. As soon as a factor of absolute scale comes into play, the self-sustaining equilibrium becomes disrupted. A situation that seemed as if it could persist into the indefinite future suddenly moves on to an altogether different status.

We encounter this non-linear relationship between resource exploitation and population growth with respect to many other natural resource stocks, notably forests, soil cover, fisheries, water supplies and pollution-absorbing services of the atmosphere. Whereas resource exploitation may have been growing gradually for very long periods without any great harm, the switch in scale of exploitation induced through a phase of unusually rapid population growth can readily result in a slight initial exceeding of the sustainable yield, whereupon the debacle of resource depletion is precipitated with surprising rapidity.

TOWARDS A SUSTAINABLE FUTURE

The effort to establish a sustainable future, one capable of supporting between 11 and 14 billion people by the year 2100, will require major changes in our economic, political and social structures. This applies to all nations of the global community. Many policy options are available, especially the incorporation of population and environment concerns into national planning from start to finish.

Developed and developing countries alike can embark immediately upon this reorientation by formulating comprehensive development strategies that reflect the myriad interactions between population, natural resources, consumption and technology (in line with the I=PAT equation set out above). They can also establish analytic systems of natural resource accounting (also described above), which in turn will serve to highlight the unsustainable resource-use patterns that now tend to be the norm given the same four factors of population, natural resources, consumption and technology.

These two initiatives alone will go far to establish a sustainable future for all nations. But it is also true that developing nations face exceptional challenges of economic advancement, population growth, environmental decline and development imperatives overall.

First of all, consider two measures that will require much more collaboration on the part of developed nations vis-a-vis developing nations: correcting the imbalance in international trade, so that developing nations receive more efficient and equitable prices for their exports together with greater access to major markets; and immediate relief for the international debt burden.

At the same time, developing nations can engage in basic reforms to emphasize the sustainable management of natural resources – in conjunction, of course, with comprehensive population planning. It is only by integrating environment and population factors into planning strategies that developing nations can hope to balance their ever growing populations with their natural resource base. It is also vital that such policy initiatives be integrated throughout government systems, rather than being assigned to individual ministries (often at odds with each other over planning priorities and budgets). In turn, this will enable coordinated efforts to formulate policies and programmes to conserve soils, water, forests, watersheds and coastal zones and to expand family planning services and maternal and child health care nationwide. All of these policy initiatives are prerequisites for a sustainable future.

In concert with these measures, developing-world governments should undertake two further sets of initiatives that often receive scant attention. First, they should enable local communities to exercise greater control over decisions affecting their own welfare. If governments are to make progress with such problems as depletion of natural resources, faltering food production and rural-urban migration, they should direct more emphasis to grassroots' needs as perceived by local people.

Second, developing-world governments should recognize the role of women on the environmental front. Women often play a pivotal part in managing environmental resources, yet all too often this function is over-looked by development strategies. In sub-Saharan Africa, for example, women often produce up to 75 per cent of food grown for domestic consumption,[15] and they are responsible for much soil conservation and tree planting among other environmental activities. So development strategies should take account of women's efforts to safeguard local resources. In those countries where governments have recognized the crucial contribution of women, natural resources tend to be utilized more sustainably, and in some cases environmental degradation has been reversed.[8]

Thus it is imperative that women's status be improved through more opportunities for education and employment, and especially for access to maternal and child health care in conjunction with family planning services. Where governments have improved the status of women, as in Zimbabwe, for instance, birth rates have come down.

Finally, it is evident that prospects for developing countries to make solid gains as regards population and environment issues will be at least partially contingent on major macro-economic forces that can either help or hinder their progress. To a considerable extent this will require more collaboration on the part of developed nations to provide immediate relief for the international debt burden, as well as efforts to correct imbalances in international trade, so that developing countries receive more efficient and fair prices for their exports, plus improved access to major markets.

To conclude, we know what to do in order to set ourselves on the track towards a sustainable future. The scientific understanding is there, the relevant technologies are available, the economic analyses are in place; the policy imperatives are established. In addition, we have plenty of specific experience to demonstrate we can succeed when we apply ourselves to the challenge. What is generally missing is the political will to get on with the task. But this may well reflect an inadequate grasp of the concealed costs of inaction on the part of political leaders together with the many positive payoffs that will stem from incisive and timely initiatives. In the next two chapters, we shall take a detailed look at the problems and the opportunities in the interconnected spheres of population and environment.

Some success in Zimbabwe

During the past decade, Zimbabwe has made impressive efforts to bring down its population growth rate. The country's population is growing by around 3.1 per cent a year, doubling its numbers every 23 years. The government has launched a nationwide family planning programme. Modern contraceptive use has risen rapidly: from 14 per cent in 1982 to nearly 30 per cent today. The programme, however, relies heavily on only one form of contraception – the pill. Nearly 85 per cent of all women practising some form of birth control use it.

One reason for the success of the Zimbabwean programme is that birth spacing is a deeply rooted tradition in the country, making family planning practices more acceptable. Several other factors contributed: government decentralization which permits village "development committees" to implement new programmes as they see fit; and an excellent road and health network throughout the country. In addition, the Zimbabwean government actively encourages the use of contraceptives, and because of this policy it is able to attract international support.

When the government took over management of the Zimbabwe National Family Planning Council from the International Planned Parenthood Federation (IPPF) in 1981, political commitment was also translated into funding – the programme currently operates on an annual budget of $10.5 million.

Priorities for the 1990s

For Zimbabwe to reduce its total fertility rate significantly, limiting the size of families rather than birth spacing will have to become the main reason for using contraception. The total fertility rate is still six children per woman, too high according to government planners struggling to balance a growing population with available resources. If modern contraceptives are simply taken as a replacement for traditional methods of birth spacing, the prevalence levels will not mean a lowering of the number of children per family, and the fertility transition will not be made.

Increasing the range and use of contraceptives, decreasing the size of families, and implementing other related measures (improving the role and status of women, adopting a population policy, and exploring non-clinic based delivery of services) are major priorities for the next decade. In achieving these goals, under-served groups such as adolescents, remote rural populations and poor urban dwellers living in squatter settlements and shanty towns have to be reached with family planning information and services. Zimbabwe is now placing emphasis on making contraception commonplace and on reaching segments of the population which still lack access to family planning and maternal and child health care services.

CHAPTER 2

POPULATION IMPACTS ON ENVIRONMENT, NATURAL RESOURCES AND QUALITY OF LIFE

In this chapter, three categories of population impacts are examined, in accord with the substantive themes of the 1992 Conference on Environment and Development: global issues, natural resources and quality of life. For the sake of focusing on issues that highlight the global dimension, the first part of this analysis is confined to two specific items: global warming and ozone-layer depletion.

GLOBAL ISSUES

Global warming
As has been made plain by the recent reports of the Intergovernmental Panel on Climate Change (IPCC),[30] and by numerous other extensive analyses,[31,32,33] the buildup of so-called greenhouse gases in the atmosphere appears set to bring on a phenomenon of global warming. Because the processes and mechanisms have been dealt with at length on other occasions, there is no need to reiterate them here. Rather, we shall examine the linkages to population growth (in conjunction, of course, with attendant issues such as energy demand and environmentally disruptive technology), and try to determine how much of the problem is due to the population factor.

Worldwide emissions of carbon dioxide, the gas that causes half the greenhouse effect, are estimated to have risen from 2.4 billion tonnes in 1950 to at least 6.8 billion tonnes in 1985, an average increase of 3.1 per cent a year.[34] During the same period world population grew by an average of 1.9 per cent a year. The rest of the increase, 1.2 per cent per person a year on average, ostensibly derived from higher per capita consumption of goods that involve production of carbon dioxide plus changes in technology. According to this reckoning, population growth was responsible for almost two thirds of the increase in carbon dioxide emissions.[34]

An analysis along these lines is useful as an indicative assessment. It serves to point up that population growth has indeed played a sizable role. If there had been no population growth, there would have been far less buildup of carbon dioxide. But how much less? Is it precisely the amount suggested by the calculation above? What if economic

Greenhouse gases

Five gases are responsible for the bulk of global warming.

- **Low-level ozone**, produced by a combination of nitrogen oxides and hydrocarbons (mostly from vehicle exhausts) in the presence of sunlight and oxygen, accounts for around 10 per cent of the warming.
- **Chlorofluorocarbons** – also the main cause of ozone layer depletion – account for perhaps 20 per cent of global warming. These are used in refrigeration and air conditioning, aerosols, packaging and foams.
- **Nitrous oxide**, accounting for 6 per cent, is emitted by humus decomposing rapidly after forest clearance, and by the breakdown of nitrogen fertilizers.
- **Methane** accounts for 14 per cent of global warming. Two thirds of emissions are from man-made sources. Half of these come from decomposition in irrigated fields and the guts of livestock.
- **Carbon dioxide** is responsible for around 50 per cent of all global warming. Carbon is naturally recycled between atmosphere, ocean, rocks and the biosphere. What has upset the natural balance is the burning of huge quantities of fossil fuels and massive deforestation, releasing carbon normally locked up in today's forests and in the mineralized remains of prehistoric plant life.

growth patterns had worked out differently, with alternative levels of demand for fossil fuel energy – especially insofar as a greater proportion of the reduced growth would presumably have taken place in industrialized nations? What if the growth in energy demand and the technology deployed to meet it had worked out in a manner that meant greater per capita consumption because of shifts in pricing patterns and trends, for example? There are a host of these "what if" questions that can be raised about the analysis, showing that the connection is far from clear. Moreover, it says nothing about the sectors of the world populace that have been contributing more than others. A disaggregated analysis would present a much more revealing picture.

These qualifications notwithstanding, the analysis is specially helpful when we consider the future outlook.[34,35] If carbon dioxide emissions in developing countries continue to grow at the rate of the past 40 years, they will more than double from the 1985 per capita level of 0.8 tonnes to 1.7 tonnes by 2025 – by which time these countries' populations are projected to have almost doubled from 3.7 billion people in 1985 to 7.2 billion people. This population increase would hence produce an additional 5.78 billion tonnes of carbon dioxide, a total to be compared with the present worldwide total of 6.9 billion tonnes. Of course, this reckoning implies a linear progression of patterns and trends in consumption, lifestyles and so on, whereas economic processes alone are subject to all manner of non-linear changes. All the same, the analysis serves to point up the exceptional potential for global warming inherent in the twin population factors of large human numbers and their rapid rate of increase.

The point about future population growth is exemplified in the case of India. With a current per capita income of only $330 a year – about one sixtieth that of the United States – India's electricity capacity today is only 55,000 megawatts, about twice that of New York State. Although the country possesses meagre coal reserves, it is exploiting them so fast that it now ranks as the world's fourth largest coal burner. In 1950, its coal use was only 33 million tonnes but, by 1989, it had soared to 191 million tonnes. At the same time, production of crude oil, another fossil fuel, rose from 0.3 million tonnes to 30.4 million tonnes; and total power generation increased from 5 billion kilowatt hours to 217 billion kilowatt hours.[36] The government plans a number of energy-based initiatives for development; for instance, to supply electricity to half the houses in the country. This goal alone will require the production of an additional 80,000 megawatts of power, compared with the present total capacity of 55,000 megawatts. It is anticipated that this measure, together with other development plans, will shortly induce a doubling of India's carbon emissions.[31,36]

Within this context, a paramount factor lies with population, both its size and growth rate. India's population of 853 million people in 1990, growing at 2.1 per cent a year, is projected to reach slightly more than a billion by the year 2000 and 1.4 billion by 2020. Even with its low per capita income (the A factor of the $I = PAT$ equation), and its less-than-advanced technological capacity (the T factor), India's huge population (the P factor) makes for a disproportionately large potential contribution to global warming. But suppose India managed to reduce its fertility rate to replacement level (almost half the present number of children per completed family) within the next three to four decades; and suppose that at the same time it did no more than double its per capita use of commercial energy (roughly matching that of China today), using coal. This increase, given the multiplier effect of the huge present population and its rate of growth, would result in India's emitting carbon dioxide at an annual per capita rate of one tonne by 2024, or roughly the world average in 1990. Because of the population factor, this would still be more than enough to cancel out the benefits of a putatively extreme step elsewhere, such as the termination forthwith of all coal burning on the part of the United States without replacing it with any other carbon-containing fuel.[23]

Overall, developing countries produce about 30 per cent of worldwide emissions of carbon dioxide today, while possessing 77 per cent of the world's population. Projections of recent trends to the year 2025 indicate that developing countries could then be accounting for 64 per cent of all emissions (which then would be much larger in total), while possessing 85 per cent of the world's population (according to the medium-variant projection for population growth).[37] But if the global population total in 2025 were to be held to the low projection of 6.3 billion instead of the medium projection of 7.2 billion, and supposing there were to be no reduction in per capita carbon dioxide emissions, total emissions would be reduced by 1.3 billion tonnes.[34]

Putting a brake on population growth could have even greater benefit as concerns a more potent greenhouse gas, methane, with a rate of increase higher than that for carbon dioxide. Half of all anthropogenic emissions of methane come from rice paddies, among other irrigated lands, and from ruminant livestock. These two sources have expanded mainly to meet the food needs of more people, but also because of the demand for improved diets. Irrigated lands have increased by 1.9 per cent a year since 1970, roughly the same as the rate of population growth; cattle numbers have grown by 0.9 per cent a year, less than half as much. The greatest expansion by far has occurred in developing countries in line with their need to feed fast-growing populations. Their rates of methane emissions cannot be readily reduced (by contrast with the case for carbon dioxide) on the grounds that they do not reflect wasteful consumption. Rather, they are likely to keep on expanding to keep pace with population growth. The IPCC report projects a 45 per cent increase in meat and dairy production by 2025, with a parallel increase in methane emissions.[30] While there are a few technological adaptations that could eventually help the situation, the most practical way to reduce the rise in methane emissions from these two sources in the long run is by slowing the growth in human numbers.[34]

There is a further aspect to the population-global warming connection that is still more significant. It relates to the prospects for agriculture and food supplies in a greenhouse-affected world. Recent research and analysis have generated a model that calculates population size, and the production, consumption and storage of grain under different climate scenarios over a 20-year period.[38] Grain supplies over half of the calories in an average diet when consumed directly, and a substantial part of the remainder when consumed in the form of meat, eggs and dairy products; one tonne of grain a year can provide four adults with adequate diets and five adults with subsistence diets. Grain also accounts for the vast majority of international trade in food. According to the model cited, each one tonne deficit in grain production results in two deaths – a distinctly conservative calculation.

The model postulates an entirely plausible greenhouse scenario for early next century, one that foresees a possible 10 per cent reduction in the global grain harvest on average three times a decade (the 1988 droughts in just the United States, Canada and China resulted in almost a 5 per cent decline). Given the way the world's food reserves have dwindled to almost nothing in recent years as a result of droughts and poor land management, it is not unrealistic to reckon that each such grain harvest shortfall would result in the starvation deaths of between 50 and 400 million people.

In addition, global warming may well reduce croplands by as much as a third (within a range of 10 to 50 per cent), because of increased temperatures and reduced rainfall plus coastal flooding.[31,33,39-42] Global warming's impact could be specially severe in developing lands of the tropics, since they tend to be more vulnerable to climatic change. Moreover, developing countries have next to no food reserves for the most part, and their citizens often subsist on marginal diets already. Worst of all, these countries have all too limited capital and infrastructure with which to adapt to changes in climate. Yet according to the 1990 IPCC report,[30] the regions that appear to be at greatest risk of extreme climatic dislocations for agriculture are often those where marginal environments sometimes make agriculture an insecure enterprise already: the Sahel, southern Africa, the Indian sub-continent, eastern Brazil and Mexico. Latest climatic models show patterns of drought increasing in frequency from 5 per cent of the time under the present climate to 50 per cent by the year 2050.[30,39]

On top of all this, the leading grain producers in the developed world are North America, the Soviet Union, Europe and Australia, accounting for about 43 per cent of global grain production. Yet precisely these countries, with the possible exception of the parts of Soviet Union, could well incur relatively more severe climatic consequences in a greenhouse-affected world.[43] Even if one allows for a "fertilizer effect" on grain production as a consequence of enhanced carbon dioxide levels in the atmosphere, leading to 5 to 10 per cent increases in grain production every 3 to 5 years, this does not prevent the projected deaths of over 800 million people during a 20-year period.

Yet another adverse repercussion is expected to arise from global warming, again with a strong relationship to population growth. It concerns environmental refugees and the impact of rising sea level on human communities in developing countries with large and dense populations.[44-48] This will be taken up later.

Ozone-layer depletion

The second global issue to be considered is ozone-layer depletion. Again, the causes and mechanisms, together with the impacts on human health, agriculture and marine ecosystems, have been dealt with at length in numerous studies.[49-52] So there is no need to cover those basic aspects here, except to note that on top of human health repercussions such as increased cancers and eye cataracts, there will be adverse consequences for a good number of crop plants on land and sea-based phytoplankton food chains. Rather, we shall look at linkages with population.

The developing world, with only a tenth of the developed world's per capita consumption of the main ozone-depleting chemicals, chlorofluorocarbons (CFCs), currently produces only about 17 per cent of the global total. But if current trends were to be maintained, the developing world's production of CFCs would reach 29 per cent of the global output as early as 2000. Much of the growing demand is centred on refrigerators, this being the largest and fastest-growing use of CFCs in developing countries. India alone plans to provide 300 million refrigerators by early next century.

The role of population growth in consumption and production of CFCs is illustrated by the case of China which intends to increase significantly its stock of refrigerators, preferably utilizing CFCs. To date only one Chinese household in 10 possesses a refrigerator. The government plans a nationwide effort to increase the proportion, along the lines of the Beijing experience during the 1980s where the proportion soared from less than 3 per cent to more than 60 per cent. China has built 12 CFC production plants in order to accommodate the refrigerator needs of many more of today's 250 million households. The government has been planning that by the year 2000 the nation would expand CFC production 10-fold, which would still leave per capita output at only one fifth that of the United States. But China's vast human numbers – 1.16 billion today, growing by 17 million a year – make the CFC impact a critically determining factor. Fortunately, both China and India have recently indicated their readiness to join in the Montreal and Helsinki initiatives to reduce CFC production.

NATURAL RESOURCES

To what extent are natural resources, concentrating on agricultural lands, water, forests and biological diversity, affected by population growth? And how far does degradation of these resources affect population questions? How do they all link in with the imperative of sustainable development?

Agricultural lands

After three and a half decades of increasing food output per capita, the world has now experienced several years of "plateauing" in crop yields. Much of the problem lies with degradation of agricultural lands after decades-long overloading of the natural resource base, due in part to population pressures. As much as 70,000 square kilometres of farmland are abandoned each year as a result of degradation, while another 200,000 square kilometres lose virtually all their agricultural productivity.[53,54]

Soil erosion is one of the chief forms of land degradation.[53,55-59] Unchecked soil erosion could well cause a decline of 19 to 29 per cent in food production from rainfed croplands during the 25 years from 1985 to 2010.[60] The problem is due to several factors apart from population growth, notably poverty: impoverished peasants cannot afford the conservation measures needed to protect soil cover. At the same time, population growth serves to induce farmers to over-use and even exhaust the soil. Thus, it often happens that agricultural yields are expanded to meet population growth's demand in the short term, but at a cost to soil cover and fertility that eventually results in declining agricultural productivity.

Consider, for illustration, the case of Java. The population has surged from 51 million in 1950 to 112 million today; 62 per cent of the nation's total population is now located on 8 per cent of its national territory. This rapid buildup in human numbers has served to aggravate soil erosion. In 44,000 square kilometres of upland farming areas, the population density has reached a level of 700 to 900 persons per square kilometre, even 2,000 persons or more in some localities, while the average land holding has declined to a mere 0.7 of a hectare. One third of these upland areas are seriously eroding, and more than 10,000 square kilometres of grainlands have been degraded to the point they no longer support even subsistence farming. This threatens the livelihood of 12 million people, many of whom live in absolute poverty and have no means to engage in soil-conservation practices. [61-64]

Desertification is an even more severe form of land degradation.[65-69] This process is estimated to be threatening 45 million square kilometres or a full third of the Earth's land surface – together with the livelihoods of at least 850 million people, of whom 135 million are experiencing the rigours of severe desertification. Already it eliminates 60,000 square kilometres of agricultural land each year, and impoverishes another 200,000 square kilometres, reducing yields and requiring costly remedial measures. The costs in terms of agricultural output forgone are estimated to be in the order of $30 billion a year. One of the main causes of desertification is over-grazing by domestic livestock. Yet the IPCC Working Group III report projects a 45 per cent increase in meat and dairy output by 2025, largely to cater to population growth and dietary upgrading.[30] In the absence of unexpectedly productive breakthroughs in technology, this implies a marked increase in livestock numbers.

As in the case of soil erosion, desertification stems in part from faulty agricultural policies, lack of extension services and inadequate attention to subsistence agriculture, among other adverse factors. In part too, it arises from exogenous factors such as the international trading system and foreign debt that induce a number of countries to engage in cash-crop-for-export agriculture rather than food-producing agriculture.[70,71] At the height of the Sahel droughts, several countries were exporting more peanuts and cotton than ever before.[72]

But population growth plays a salient part as well, through the phenomenon of the marginal peasant impelled into marginal (too dry) environments.[73] Moreover, population growth is generally higher in semi-arid and arid lands than elsewhere. In over half of the 34 predominantly dry countries (those in which more than three quarters of total area is dry), population growth has been 3 per cent or more since the mid-1970s.[74,75] Because it is usually too difficult to increase productivity on established croplands with their dryness (there has been much less of an increase in agricultural productivity in the drier regions of Africa and the Middle East than in Latin America and South/Southeast Asia), the main agricultural response has been to expand the area cultivated. Feeding additional people would be taxing to a degree even without drought and desertification. The problem, in turn, has served to trigger some of the most broad-scale migrations in recent decades.

These two instances of land degradation (soil erosion and desertification) show that the problem is due in significant degree to lack of socio-economic infrastructure for agriculture and especially in support of its resource base. In turn, this includes a lengthy list of factors, such as perverse pricing practices, inadequate credit and marketing facilities, over-regulation on the part of governments, and a general policy emphasis in favour of the urban-industrial sector to the detriment of the rural-agricultural sector.[76] All these serve, both directly and indirectly, to exacerbate degradation.

The impact of population growth, especially the absolute increase in human numbers each year, also plays a substantive part in land degradation. In principle, it would be possible through improved agricultural policies, agro-technologies and the like, to safeguard the food resource base and to make it still more productive. But the experience of the 1980s, when population growth became an ever more prominent factor, shows that agricultural lands have been deteriorating and per capita food production declining in much of southern Asia, sub-Saharan Africa and the Andean countries.[5,58] Agronomic strategies assume stability in the environmental state of the resource base, whereas the reverse is true in many agricultural areas. There are all too few instances where new technologies for soil conservation and crop management have kept pace with the demands of surging human numbers. On the contrary, productive capacity has been declining steadily in entire regions.

To cater to increased food needs in the future we should theoretically plan for a 50 per cent increase in cultivated lands in developing countries by 2025.[23,77] Yet, the principal food areas, grainlands, have not increased since 1981, following a 24 per cent expansion from 1950. Instead, they have been contracting as the amount of land opened up has not kept pace with the amount taken out of production because of land degradation. Indeed, the world average of per capita cropland has been decreasing at a rate that, if continued, will leave only half as much in 2000 as in 1950.[78]

Overall, land degradation of various sorts has been estimated by the Worldwatch Institute to be causing an annual loss of roughly 14 million tonnes of grain output.[5] This translates into almost half of all gains in grain output each year. It means the overall net increase in grain output is reduced to less than 1 per cent a year – while population growth amounts to almost 2 per cent a year. In turn, this translates into rising grain prices as reserve grain stocks have fallen to little more than "pipeline supplies": between 1986 and 1989 rice prices rose 38 per cent and wheat prices 48 per cent.[5] The 1980s have seen little expansion of croplands because there is little suitable land left to mobilize for arable agriculture, and there appears to be less scope than in the past for intensification of food production through expanding irrigation. So the environmental constraint of land degradation, worth 14 million tonnes of grain a year, could soon become all the more constraining, in that the world needs an additional 28 million tonnes of grain output a year just to keep up with population growth, let alone to upgrade nutrition and to meet demands from increasing affluence.[5]

In short, it is now becoming apparent there has been an environment-population debacle building up for decades in the agricultural sector, covert and largely disregarded until the last few years. Worse, it looks as if it has the makings of a major crisis during the 1990s. Suppose the rate of grain-output increase continues the 1985-onwards pattern of falling behind population growth, and that technological responses, plus related responses such as increased investment in agriculture, keep on proving incapable (as they did for much of the 1980s) of supplying the responses that boosted grain output for all of three decades from 1950 onwards. Whatever the present problems of land degradation (they appear set to grow worse if only because of the cumulative impacts of farmers' long-term overloading of their croplands), they will be grossly aggravated by the compounding impact of population growth with an additional 900 million people in the developing world during the 1990s. So the decade ahead could see a combination of mounting grain deficits, surging grain prices and spreading hunger among ever larger numbers of people.

This mega-problem will hit hardest at those least capable of withstanding it, the world's bottom billion poorest people or precisely those who generally feature the highest fertility rates. Thus, the agricultural-lands problem will keep on being compounded by the predominant and most persistent factor of all, population growth. The shrinking size of landholdings in many areas of the developing world is a direct result of rapid population growth, combined with poor agricultural practices, lack of rural infrastructure and inadequate government policies among other factors.

Take Nepal as an example. In this mountainous, rugged country, farmsteads are already small, since steep slopes are prone to soil erosion. As the population growth rate remains high (2.3 per cent a year), there are more sons to inherit shares of ever smaller plots of land. The average size of upland farms has been reduced from 3 to 4 hectares 30 years ago to barely a hectare today. In the over-crowded plains along the Indian border, farms are so tiny – one third of a hectare – that farmers can no longer make a living from the land. This forces the poorer farmers to open up marginal land on steep slopes, to cut down watershed forests and to misuse water supplies. Even precipitously steep slopes have been planted with maize and wheat. Yet, in many areas, yields remain low and livelihoods continue to erode with the soils.[79]

Kenya too faces severe land fragmentation because of rapid population growth. The average amount of land per person has fallen from 0.4 hectares in 1969, to 0.2 hectares today. As in Nepal, poorer farmers are forced into marginal areas where soils wear out fast and yields remain low.[15] Many landholdings in Kenya and elsewhere are already too small to provide an adequate living. Large numbers have been turned into part-time farms, with the wife and children staying at home to tend crops while the husband migrates in search of wage employment. Or the land is simply sold off to larger and richer landowners, making landholdings still more unequal and creating a still larger pool of landless labourers. This process applies in many other developing countries. In practice, for the children of the poor, large families mean smaller landholdings today and landlessness tomorrow. With no prospect of rural employment, many of the destitute migrate to towns and cities. Land reform offers a partial solution, but it is an option few countries have undertaken successfully.[1]

With much land degradation stemming from excessive population pressures, the most productive way to reverse the situation surely lies with a rapid reduction in population growth. Otherwise, the prospect is that Africa's over-burdened lands will need to support an extra 225 million people and India's an extra 189 million people by the year 2000.

Water

Water is an eminently renewable resource in principle. Its stocks can be recharged either through natural hydrological cycles or through human-directed means. Yet all too often, it is utilized as a non-renewable resource.[80-88] Furthermore, natural circumstances rarely make water available in the right amount at the right place at the right time. In many parts of the developing world, human communities experience almost continuous shortages of water: already as many as 2 billion people live in areas with chronic shortages.[89] To make matters worse, the demand for water in several parts of the world is increasing more rapidly than population numbers, owing to rising standards of living.

Water and disease. As a measure of water problems in the public-health sector alone, the proportion of human communities with ready access to safe drinking water in 1984 was a mere 19 per cent in Sri Lanka; 18 per cent in Paraguay; 16 per cent in Uganda; 14 per cent in Sierra Leone; 13 per cent in Mozambique; 11 per cent in Nepal; 10 per cent in Afghanistan; 6 per cent in Mali and 4 per cent in Ethiopia – to cite but the worst placed countries.[90] Between 1970 and 1984, the number of developing-world inhabitants without access to clean water or adequate sanitation increased by 135 million, almost entirely because of population growth. In several dry regions – not only the Middle East but North Africa and the Sahel – as much as 50 per cent (a crucial level) of stable runoff from rivers is already being used, with adverse consequences for public health supplies.

The significance of these figures is reflected in the developing-world incidence of infectious diseases. In water-short communities, household needs are supplied by local streams, lakes and irrigation channels, many of which are contaminated by pollutants and human excreta. Water-borne pathogens – which contribute in particular to typhoid, cholera, amoebic infections, bacillary dysentery and diarrhoea – account for 80 per cent of all disease in developing countries, and for 90 per cent of the 13 million child deaths each year. Directly, this has a horrendous impact on the attainment of desired family size, whereas indirectly it prompts couples to have even larger numbers of children just to compensate for the premature deaths of their children.

Water-related disease is particularly acute in urban communities. In 1985, at least 25 per cent of urban communities (and 58 per cent of rural communities) were without clean water for sanitation needs. As the countryside around cities like Manila and Panama City loses its tree cover, so too the domestic water supplies decline in quantity and quality. In turn, human communities face a growing threat of contaminated-water pandemics. Similarly, public-health programmes in Bangkok, Nairobi, Lagos and Abidjan, among other conurbations of the humid tropics, are being set back because their water supplies are declining in the wake of deforestation in upland catchments. Peninsular Malaysia has some of the highest rainfall in the world, yet water has regularly been rationed for part of the year in Kuala Lumpur and several other urban areas.[91] Water demand in the Peninsula is expected to double between 1985 and 2000; and if per capita water supplies decline, costs will increase even more rapidly for the Malaysian consumer.

Water for irrigation. Irrigated croplands, which now constitute about 18 per cent of all arable lands and produce 33 per cent of all food, account for 65 per cent of water use worldwide.[92,25] Since 1950, these lands have increased from 940,000 square kilometres to 2.7 million square kilometres, an expansion that has been responsible for about half of the world's increased output of food. More than half of all today's irrigated lands are in developing countries. If we are to grow twice as much food during the next two decades, as we must if we are to keep up with population growth and nutritional demands, at least half of the increase is planned to come from irrigated croplands. But, whereas the rate of expansion of area irrigated grew during the 1960s and 1970s by 2 to 4 per cent a year, it declined to only about 1 per cent a year during the 1980s.[85] In fact, with a net gain in irrigated land of less than 240,000 square kilometres during the 1980s, and with an increase in population of almost a billion, the supply of irrigation water per person declined by 8 per cent.[93] The 1980s were the first decade when both per capita irrigation water and cropland area diminished.

Furthermore, in several of the better irrigated parts of Asia, from Pakistan to the Philippines, the Green Revolution has been losing momentum as farmers can no longer rely on adequate flows of irrigation water for their multiple crops of rice each year – a deficit due in part to deforestation of watershed catchments.[58,94] Throughout the region, and especially in Pakistan, Thailand and Vietnam, also the island of Java, the largest constraint on expanding rice production may prove to be not lack of land, fertilizer, agronomic technologies and so on, but lack of irrigation water in appropriate amounts at the right time of year.[95] To cite an economist with long-term experience in the region: "Water budgets are becoming as critical to the national well-being in many Asian nations as the balance of payments and foreign exchange reserves. Great increases in water efficiency could become available through improved methods of irrigation, through land levelling, and more efficient on-farm controls. But to manage water for maximum productivity will require a planning capacity which few Asian societies have demonstrated in recent times."[96]

A similar situation holds for much of Central America. In the last quarter of this century, Costa Rica has been planning to expand its irrigated croplands by 180 per cent; El Salvador by 230 per cent; Nicaragua by 300 per cent and Panama by 340 per cent.[9] Yet in all these countries, deforestation of upland watersheds is proceeding apace, with adverse effects on river flows for valleylands with their dense human populations. Already these countries' water needs are catching up with stable runoff from watersheds. In several localities the situation is almost as critical as in much of the Indian sub-

Irrigation: the solution that became a problem

The importance of irrigation, both to feed growing numbers of people and to provide an adequate living for rural populations, cannot be overstated. In India, for example, 30 per cent of the country's cultivated land is under some form of irrigation, producing an impressive 55 per cent of the food output. Fifty per cent of China's croplands are irrigated, producing 70 per cent of all the food consumed. A combination of improved seed varieties and irrigation made the "Green Revolution" possible in Asia. The world's irrigated croplands account for the lion's share of freshwater used every year – 73 per cent of total water withdrawals. Worldwide, irrigation covers about 271 million hectares and the area is expanding.

But a disturbing trend is emerging wherever irrigation is used. The United Nations Food and Agriculture Organization (FAO) estimates that half of the total area of irrigated cropland may be in danger from three "silent enemies" – salinization, alkalization and waterlogging.

Every year, around 1.5 million hectares of mostly prime agricultural land is salinized and taken out of production. In the United States alone, it is thought that 20 to 25 per cent of all irrigated land (some 4 million hectares) is affected. And it is a persistent problem in the plains of eastern and western China, the Indian sub-continent, Central Asia and Asia Minor, the Aral-Caspian lowlands, the Caucasus and southeastern Europe, the Middle East, North and West Africa and the plains of South America.

In India, where 40 million hectares were irrigated in 1982 (half by surface water, half by wells) more than 7 million hectares were affected by salinity and alkalinity and could no longer support any agricultural activities. Even more alarming, waterlogged areas are counted among those lands defined as "water-eroded" and currently amount to a staggering 73 million hectares out of India's total agricultural area of 143 million hectares.

These three silent enemies of irrigated agriculture are not easy to detect until they reach a crisis level. Even the best irrigation water from rivers or aquifers still contains salts and alkalis. Supplying 10,000 cubic metres of water deposits in the soil 2 to 5 tonnes of salt per hectare of land. After 10 to 20 years of continuous irrigation without proper drainage, salts and alkaline materials in the soil accumulate to toxic proportions in the root zones of the crops, effectively "sterilizing" the soil. This process is often complicated by waterlogging, since the water has no place to go but down. It sinks into the soil, gradually raising the water table and waterlogging the crop roots. Under such conditions, yields fall and eventually agricultural production becomes impossible.

Currently, most irrigation efficiencies are a travesty of mis-management. In many areas farmers tend to over-irrigate because of low (or non-existent) prices for water and the use of cheap gravity systems. As a result, it is not uncommon for 70 to 80 per cent of the water withdrawn from a river for irrigation purposes never to reach its intended destination. It runs off before reaching the crops, sinks into unlined canals, or is evaporated before it can be used. Even in the Colorado River Basin in the southwestern United States, the efficiency of water use is below 50 per cent.

In a different but related sequence, unsustainable use of groundwater for irrigation and other uses has depleted supplies and lowered water tables. The final stage is land subsidence, which is now a major problem in 42 areas around the world. In the Indian State of Tamil Nadu, the water table has dropped 25 to 30 metres in one decade. In China, 50 cities are threatened by water shortages and the water table beneath Beijing is sinking by up to two metres a year (a third of its wells have dried up from over-use).

The silent enemies are less of a problem where farmers can afford to rehabilitate damaged croplands. But in developing countries – particularly in Asia and Africa – land restoration is either too costly, or technologically beyond reach. Prevention is the only answer.

Prevention depends on making farmers responsible for the water they use, by pricing or rationing it. It demands education, as well as services and training at the community level, to encourage sustainable irrigation systems and to manage them properly once they are in place.

continent. A parallel situation exists in Africa along a broad belt bordering the tropical forests of the equatorial zone and the strip along the Gulf of Guinea, where irrigated agriculture is expected to encounter water shortages in several countries before the year 2000.

"Water stress". Water consumption has doubled at least twice this century, and demand could well double again during the next two decades, primarily because of population growth. Yet in 88 developing countries with 40 per cent of the world's population, water deficits are already a serious constraint on development.[98,84] How much this is due to population growth *per se* is difficult to determine precisely since advancing technology often feeds demand while also offering scope for repeated reuse of what should be an intrinsically renewable resource. But in general terms, it is plausible to argue there is a sizable contribution to the problem from rapid population growth in conjunction with lack of socio-economic infrastructure – this latter factor being, as we have seen in Chapter 1, a

reflection of population pressures on limited development resources.

   According to a pioneering analysis by Swedish hydrologist Dr. Malin Falkenmark,[99] a society typically experiences "water stress" when the number of people competing for each annual "flow unit" of a million cubic metres of water reaches 2,000, in other words, 500 cubic metres per person. After this point it is almost certain there will be inherent water-deficit problems, often acute scarcity and even outright shortages. This ultimate "water barrier" level also applies in countries with advanced technology and administrative capability. In developing countries with less socio-economic infrastructure, the barrier may come into play at a level a good deal lower, especially if annual seasonality or periodic droughts are significant.[81-83] In some countries the barrier appears to be significant when only 1,000 people compete for each flow unit.

   By the end of this decade most countries in North Africa and in East Africa are projected to exceed the 2,000-persons measure of scarcity, five of them having less than 1,000 cubic metres of water per person. Most of these have annual population growth rates exceeding 2.5 per cent. It must be stressed that this does not mean that high population growth rates cause *per se* the entire problem, since several

WATER SCARCITY INDEX IN SELECTED AFRICAN COUNTRIES

Country	Population* (millions)			Renewable supply of terrestrial water systems (cubic kilometres per year)	Level of water consumption (people per million cubic metres per year)		
	1982	2000	2025		1982	2000	2025
Algeria	20	35	57	31	650	1,100	1,900
Burundi	5	7	11	4	1,200	1,900	3,100
Egypt	44	69	97	95	460	690	1,000
Kenya	18	39	83	37	480	1,000	2,200
Malawi	7	12	23	9	730	1,300	2,600
Morocco	22	36	60	32	680	1,100	1,900
Nigeria	82	162	338	308	270	530	1,100
Rwanda	5	11	22	6	810	1,680	3,500
Somalia	5	7	13	12	430	600	1,100
Tanzania	19	39	84	76	250	520	1,100
Tunisia	7	10	14	5	1,500	2,100	3,000
Zimbabwe	8	15	33	23	350	660	1,400

* Population figures in this table are based on an earlier estimation and, as such, do not correspond to latest figures.

countries concerned lie in semi-arid or arid zones where water scarcity is an enduring problem anyway. But it is difficult to see how more water can be mobilized fast enough through recycling and other efforts in order to support agriculture for burgeoning populations that are largely projected to double within a generation at most. Sub-Saharan Africa is exceptionally short of skilled manpower, technical skills and other forms of socio-economic infrastructure to make more sustained use of available water supplies. In short, population growth with its compounding impacts serves to make a severe problem a super-problem.

This last factor, with its feedback effects, illustrates the question of an emergent "risk spiral" concerning water resources.[81,83,100] Driven by population growth and fuelled by hydro-climatic factors (the one reinforces the other's impact), the phenomenon of accelerating water shortages argues for greater attention to be directed at a resource-scarcity problem that could eventually match parallel problems of food and energy. Still further population-derived feedbacks could come into play as growing human numbers engender land degradation, which then leads to disruption of watershed flows, compounding irregularities of water supplies.

The case of Egypt. An extreme case of water shortages is manifested by Egypt, where virtually all croplands depend on irrigation. Two decades ago Egypt was self-sufficient in food but, today, because of a combination of population growth, land shortages and poor planning, the nation experiences fast-mounting difficulties in feeding itself.[101] In 1986, the nation had to import 10.8 million tonnes of cereal grains, or 55 per cent of its food needs, at a cost of $4.1 billion. This amount could well double by the year 2000, when Egypt's 1990 population of 52 million is projected to reach 64 million. Egypt's external debt reached $44 billion in 1988; service of non-military debt alone consumes around 30 per cent of export earnings. If Egypt cannot reduce its debt through increased trade revenues (in recent years its terms of trade have steadily declined), it may not be able to buy all the grain it needs.

What prospect, then, that Egypt can grow more food of its own? Due primarily to rapid population growth but also to environmental problems, grain output per person declined between 1970-72 and 1985 by 18 per cent.[102] Of a million square kilometres of national territory, only 25,000 square kilometres are cultivated, in a strip averaging 10 kilometres wide along the River Nile. Farming is critically dependent on irrigation, but by 1982 half of all irrigated croplands were suffering some degree of salinization, and all the rest were considered at risk.[103]

Today, about 10 per cent of agricultural production is lost annually to decline of soil fertility, and 8 per cent is lost to desert encroachment.

Nor are population trends encouraging. There has been hardly any reduction in the population growth rate since 1980. The 1990 rate is 2.3 per cent, meaning a doubling time of less than 30 years. With plenty of demographic momentum built into present growth trends and patterns, even a vigorous family planning campaign will have difficulty curtailing population growth for the best part of a generation – by which time the population total is likely to be twice as large as today.

In this tightly constrained situation, Egypt could face growing water shortages. Eight successive drought years in the watershed territories of Ethiopia and equatorial Africa reduced the Nile flows by mid-1988 to the lowest level since 1913. Storage water in Lake Nasser looked likely to prove enough for only the harvest of 1988. Thereafter, the early-1989 planting season could have been so curtailed through lack of irrigation water that Egypt would have had to import a further 15 per cent of its food needs for this cause alone.[104] But the upstream drought broke in August 1988, and the immediate crisis was relieved.

But were the 1980s' drought in the upstream catchments to return, as many climatologists anticipate in light of the greenhouse effect,[105] the results would be, according to Mr. Sarwat Fahamy, Director of the Nile Water Control Authority, "a calamity". The water shortages would affect not only agriculture. By mid-1988, the low flows into the Aswan Dam's hydropower turbines, which supply 40 per cent of Egypt's electricity needs, reduced power output by 20 per cent; and even before the drought, the nation was failing to meet a 10 per cent annual growth rate in demand for electricity. A new drought could easily result in a still more serious power cut than in mid-1988, even as high as 60 per cent, at a cost of millions of dollars worth of lost energy each month. Since the deficit would have to be made up with oil, the low-flows problem would all but eliminate Egypt's oil-export revenues – placing still further restrictions on Egypt's ability to buy food overseas.

Yet another and even greater threat to Egypt's water supplies is emerging. This one stems from new claims on the part of upstream nations for a greater share of the Nile's waters.[106-109] The other eight nations within the river's drainage are shifting from dependency on rainwater to irrigation systems for their croplands. This applies notably in Ethiopia, which controls the Blue Nile tributary, source of around 80 per cent of Nile water entering Egypt. Ethiopia has never joined Egypt (or the other downstream nation, Sudan) in a legal agreement to regulate the share-out of the Nile's waters. On the contrary, Ethiopia has regularly asserted that as a sovereign state it feels at complete liberty to dispose of its natural resources in whatever manner it pleases.[110,111] As a result of population growth, among other factors, the Ethiopian government is resettling 1.5 million impoverished peasants from the degraded highlands into the fertile southwestern sector. In order to supply irrigation water for the new settlements, Ethiopia plans to divert up to 39 per cent of the Blue Nile's waters before they leave its territory. Unless a water management scheme can be worked out with all riparian countries, such a move may well trigger a major resource conflict between Egypt and Ethiopia.[112,113]

Water supplies and global warming. Whatever the immediate prospect of growing water deficits in several parts of the world with both large populations and high growth rates, the long-range outlook will surely be much modified by global warming. While the issue is too complex for a detailed discussion here, suffice it to note that water scarcity induced by the greenhouse effect appears set to eliminate irrigation on 5 per cent of the world's present irrigated croplands, removing 135,000 square kilometres from the global base and requiring compensatory investments of the order of $26 to $52 billion. In addition, new investments for agriculture, notably irrigation systems, could well require some $120 to $240 billion.[93,114]

Tropical Forests

According to recent estimates,[115] tropical moist forests lost 142,200 square kilometres of their expanse during 1989. This amounted to 1.8 per cent of remaining forests, covering slightly less than 8 million square kilometres. In 1979, these forests lost 75,000 square kilometres of their expanse, so the 1989 figure represents a 90 per cent increase in the deforestation rate – deforestation here means the outright destruction of all tree cover, as distinct from degradation of forest ecosystems that nonetheless leaves some trees standing.

How much tropical deforestation can be attributed to population growth? For an exploratory and illuminating assessment,[34] consider the role of the expansion of the cropland base on the part of small-scale farmers. During the period 1971 to 1986, cropland expansion in the entire developing world amounted to an average of 0.51 per cent a year, while population growth amounted to 2.2 per cent a year and food consumption per person increased by 0.58 per cent a year. At the same time, technological innovations improved harvest yields to the extent that the area of cropland needed per head actually declined by

2.27 per cent a year. In addition, there was encroachment on tropical forests as a result of road building, growth of urban communities and the like, that can be estimated at 588,000 square kilometres during the period – which works out to 0.056 hectares per person of the population increase. Using these various analyses, one can roughly calculate that cropland encroachment on tropical forests – the main form of cropland expansion – totalled some 1.17 million square kilometres during the period, amounting to more than 90 per cent of deforestation; and of this expansion, population growth was responsible for 79 per cent, the other 21 per cent being attributable to increases in food consumption per person. This is a rough-and-ready mode of calculation. But it serves to throw preliminary light on the scope and scale of population growth's contribution to tropical deforestation.

In those countries of the humid tropics with reserves of potentially arable land – albeit with poor soils for the most part, and acutely susceptible to environmental degradation – new areas for cultivation are opened primarily at the expense of forests. In many instances, tropical forest destruction is initiated by loggers, whereas slash-and-burn cultivators and cattle ranchers move in to claim the land once it has been partially or wholly cleared of timber. Increasingly, however, slash-and-burn cultivators are arriving in such huge numbers that they are effectively penetrating the forests on their own.[115-119]

Today, the slash-and-burn cultivator operates not so much as a shifting cultivator but as a shifted cultivator; that is, the peasant who finds himself landless in traditional farming areas, and migrates to the last unoccupied public lands available where he can practise subsistence farming. He is driven into the forests by forces he is little able to understand and still less able to resist. He is no more to be blamed for torching the forest than a soldier is to be held responsible for starting a war. Populations of subsistence cultivators are often increasing at annual rates far above the rates for nationwide increase. In the province of Rondonia, Brazil, the numbers of small-scale settlers have been increasing at a rate that surpassed 15 per cent a year for much of the period since 1975, whereas the population growth rate for all Brazil averaged only 2.1 per cent.[120] There are similar mass migrations into tropical forests, albeit with lower rates of population increase, in Colombia, Ecuador, Peru, Bolivia, Côte d'Ivoire, Nigeria, India, Thailand, Vietnam, Indonesia and the Philippines. In all these instances, population growth is a significant factor in deforestation.[115]

But one must be careful not to over-simplify the situation. A host of related factors frequently operate in addition to population growth.

They include pervasive poverty among peasant communities, maldistribution of existing farmlands, inequitable land-tenure systems, inefficient agricultural technologies, insufficient political attention to subsistence farming, lack of rural infrastructure, and faulty development policies overall. In Brazil, for instance, 5 per cent of farmland owners possess 70 per cent of all farmlands, while 70 per cent cultivate only 5 per cent of farmlands – a skewed situation that is growing worse. Moreover, another 1.7 million Brazilians enter the job market each year, over half of them failing to find enough employment to support themselves, many of them joining the forest-bound migrants in search of land and livelihood. But this is not to deny that in the countries listed, population growth appears to be a prime, if not the principal, factor leading to deforestation.

There is vast scope in future population growth for still larger throngs of shifted cultivators to accelerate deforestation. By the year 2030, 80 per cent of the world's projected population of more than 8 billion people are expected to be living in tropical forest countries. This translates into 6.4 billion people, a billion more than are on Earth today. Given the demographic momentum built into the processes of population growth, and even allowing for expanded family planning programmes, population projections suggest that in those countries where economies appear likely to remain primarily agrarian, there will be progressive pressures on remaining forests, extending for decades into the future. For instance, Ecuador's population is projected to increase from 10.9 million to 24 million before it attains zero growth in about a century's time; Cameroon's from 12 million to 67 million; Côte d'Ivoire's from 12 million to 83 million; Madagascar's from 12 million to 49 million; Nigeria's from 112 million to 500 million; Myanmar's from 43 million to 97 million; India's from 871 million to 1.7 billion; Indonesia's from 188 million to 345 million; and Vietnam's from 68 million to 168 million. Unless there is a marked reduction in population growth, together with the resolution of the landless-peasant phenomenon (a prospect that appears less than promising), it is difficult to see that much forest will remain in just a few decades' time in most of the countries cited.[121]

Fuelwood. As tropical forests decline, there is a drop-off in supply of their goods and services, notably hardwood timber, fuelwood, non-wood products (oils, exudates, fibres, fruits, etc.), watershed services and climatic functions. Since there is no space to consider them all here, this analysis will review the item that affects the most people: fuelwood.

At least two thirds of developing-world people, and the great majority of rural dwellers including virtually all the poorest of the

POPULATION GROWTH IN SELECTED TROPICAL FOREST COUNTRIES

Country	Population in 1950 (millions)	Population in 1989 (millions)	Growth of population 1989 (%)
LATIN AMERICA			
Brazil	53	147	2.1
Central America	9	28	2.8
Colombia	12	32	2.0
Ecuador	3	10	2.6
The Guyanas	0.4	1	0.2
Mexico	28	87	2.2
Peru	8	21	2.1
Venezuela	5	19	2.6
ASIA			
India	358	836	2.1
Indonesia	80	181	1.9
Kampuchea	4	8	2.5
Laos	2	4	2.8
Malaysia	6	17	2.6
Myanmar (Burma)	18	41	2.1
Papua New Guinea	2	4	2.7
Philippines	21	61	2.5
Thailand	20	55	1.5
Vietnam	30	65	2.2
AFRICA			
Cameroon	5	11	3.3
Congo	1	2	3.2
Côte d'Ivoire	3	12	3.8
Gabon	0.5	1	3.5
Madagascar	4	12	3.2
Nigeria	33	105	3.3
Zaire	12	35	3.1

poor, depend on fuelwood (or its derivative, charcoal) for their primary source of energy for domestic cooking and heating. In the early 1980s, the wood share of total energy consumption in Sudan was 74 per cent; in Nigeria 82 per cent; in Tanzania 92 per cent; in Nepal 94 per cent and in Burkina Faso 96 per cent.[122]

Most fuelwood is not traded commercially, so official estimates surely underrate the volume. But according to a number of estimates, supplies in many countries increasingly fail to keep up with demand.[122-128]

Percent of population in rural areas	Population projected in 2000 (millions)	Population projected in 2020 (millions)	Projected size of stationary population (millions)	Per capita GNP 1987 (US$)
29	180	234	280	2,020
n/a	37	54	88	1,240
33	39	51	57	1,220
56	13	19	24	1,040
52	0.9	1	n/a	1,050
34	107	142	170	1,820
31	26	35	46	1,430
17	25	35	42	3,230
74	1,042	1,374	1,766	300
74	219	287	345	450
89	10	12	n/a	n/a
84	5	7	n/a	n/a
65	22	27	37	1,800
76	51	69	97	n/a
87	5	8	12	730
59	77	131	127	590
83	64	82	98	840
81	82	121	168	n/a
58	17	32	67	960
52	3	6	17	880
57	18	35	83	750
59	1.6	2.6	6	2,750
78	17	30	49	200
72	150	255	500	370
60	49	89	200	160

In 1980, some 1.2 billion people were meeting their fuelwood needs only by cutting wood faster than it was being replenished through natural growth; and 112 million people (half of them in tropical Africa) could not meet even minimum needs without over-harvesting stocks. Consumption exceeded supply by 30 per cent in Sahelian countries; by 70 per cent in the Sudan and India; by 150 per cent in Ethiopia and by 200 per cent in Niger. By the year 2000, more than half of all developing-world people, or over 2.5 billion, are projected to be gaining their supplies only by over-harvesting, and 350 million people will face absolute shortages.

POPULATION EXPERIENCING A FUELWOOD DEFICIT,
1980 AND 2000 (millions)

	Latin America	Africa	Near East and North Africa	Asia and the Pacific	Total	
1980						
Total population	26	55		31	112	Acute
Rural population	18	49		29	96	scarcity
Total population	201	146	104	832	1,283	Deficit
Rural population	143	131	69	710	1,052	
2000						Acute
Total population	512	535	268	1,671	2,986	scarcity
Rural population	342	464	158	1,434	2,398	or deficit

Eliminating the gap between projected demand and supply would have meant planting 550,000 square kilometres of high-yielding fuelwood plantations during the last two decades of this century. But actual plantings average only 5,500 square kilometres a year.[127]

Fuelwood deficits mean a greater burden in finding the daily supply. They result in under-cooked food which is less nourishing and more likely to contain pathogens than if properly prepared. Shortages also mean that women, generally the main wood gatherers, have to spend more time trekking longer distances to find wood. In parts of Nepal, it has been found that the time spent gathering fuelwood means that women's agricultural labour is reduced by 40 per cent.[129] In Tanzania, the value of fuelwood production nationwide in 1983, imputed from market prices, was 207 million Tanzanian shillings. But had an amount been included to reflect the cost of time spent in seeking fuelwood, the putative value would have risen to 2.7 billion shillings. This latter figure, plus an estimate for forest depreciation through over-harvesting of fuelwood, would have meant a reduction in the nation's Net National Product of 11 per cent.[130] Needless to say, these are rough estimates, but "creative calculation" of this kind is urgently needed if we are to assess the full consequences of fuelwood shortages.

The most significant secondary effect lies with the practice of burning livestock manure and crop residues as substitutes for fuelwood, leading to a decline in cropland fertility. In Ethiopia, for example, cattle dung production in 1981-82 could be reckoned at roughly 23 million tonnes dry weight; and in certain parts of the country, 60 to 90 per cent of the dung was burned for domestic fuel. [131] If we calculate that just under 8 million tonnes overall were used as fuel, this translates, with an average grain-response value of $76 per tonne, into agricultural output forgone worth some $600 million, or roughly 30 per cent of the country's value added in its entire agricultural sector.[132]

What is the role of population growth in all this? Again, it is not the only factor. Because fuelwood shortages tend to strike hardest at the poorest of the poor – those who are disenfranchised in political, economic, social and institutional terms – governments are disinclined to accord them as much attention as they deserve. So there is a failure of policy. Moreover, there is inadequate understanding of the seriousness of the situation in terms of its overall impact including ripple effects: another failure on the part of political leaders. Much more could have been done through afforestation and reforestation programmes and through support for alternative forms of energy, also for more efficient cooking stoves and other energy-saving technologies.

Nevertheless, sheer growth in human numbers and their needs has done much to precipitate the decades-long over-cutting that has led to the current crisis. It is population growth too that contributes in large measure to the still greater crisis ahead. In Pakistan, for instance, fuelwood supply in 1985 was 19.7 million cubic metres, while demand was 25 million cubic metres or 25 per cent higher – a reflection in part of population growth rates of 2.5 to 3 per cent a year for several decades. By the year 2000, when there will be an additional 43 million people on top of the 1985 total (a 41 per cent increase), fuelwood demand is expected to increase by 55 per cent.[123] So while there are factors at work apart from population growth (socio-economic advancement and increasing aspirations), population growth can be roughly reckoned to contribute almost 75 per cent of the expanded demand.

Generally speaking, it is among the most fuelwood-short communities of Pakistan, containing the most impoverished people, that population growth is most rapid. The causative connection between upsurge in human numbers and deficiencies in fuelwood supplies is not always tight, still less is it exclusive. But it is there; it is significant; and it is increasing fast.

TROPICAL FORESTS
AND HOT SPOT AREAS

Biological diversity

The Earth is estimated to contain at least 5 million and probably more than 30 million species, even though only 1.7 million or so have been documented. Of the total, the great majority, surely 75 per cent and possibly as many as 90 per cent or even more, are found in tropical forests.[133] So the biological diversity problem, or rather biological depletion problem, is located almost entirely in tropical forests, which, as we have just seen, are being eliminated at ever more rapid rates.

California
Floristic
Province

Colombian Chocó/
Western
Ecuador

Uplands of
Western
Amazonia

Atlantic
Coast Brazil

Central
Chile

Tropical forests

Hot spot areas

The current extinction rate has been estimated variously at between 50 and 100 species a day, with several million species facing demise by the year 2000 (assuming a planetary total of at least 30 million species), and conceivably as many as a half of all species facing extinction by the end of the next century.[23,134-138]

According to a summary calculation, the 1979 tropical deforestation rate of 0.62 per cent a year implied a species loss of 0.15 per cent a year.[138] If 79 per cent of annual deforestation is due to population growth (a large supposition, but acceptable for illustrative purposes), then 0.12 per cent of annual species losses in tropical forests can now be attributed to population growth.[34]

But this reckoning is based on a 1979 deforestation rate of 0.6 per cent a year. As we have seen, the 1989 rate is 1.8 per cent a year. So the population-induced extinction rate in tropical forests can more properly be estimated – as a crude calculation – at 0.36 per cent a year. If there are 30 million species in tropical forests, this works out to 108,000 species a year. Tentative as this figure may be, it is offered for the purpose of shedding some preliminary light on population growth's contribution to mass extinction.

An alternative assessment is available from an analysis of certain "hot spot" areas, these being areas that both feature exceptional concentrations of species with high levels of endemism (not found elsewhere), and face exceptional threats of habitat destruction. According to two sets of analysis, there are 14 such hot spots in tropical forests and 4 in Mediterranean-type zones.[134,135] Collectively, they contain almost 50,000, or 20 per cent, of Earth's plant species in 746,000 square kilometres or 0.5 per cent of Earth's land surface. Insofar as can be reasonably determined, they contain an even larger proportion of Earth's animal species. If, as is anticipated, they experience gross environmental destruction within the foreseeable future, these areas alone will witness a mass extinction greater than any in the past 65 million years. While it is not possible to indicate the precise role of population growth in the elimination of these hot-spot localities, it is plainly a key factor, if not the crucial factor, in those localities where the shifted cultivator phenomenon is paramount – northwestern Ecuador, western Amazonia, southwestern Côte d'Ivoire, eastern Tanzania, Madagascar, southwestern India, southwestern Sri Lanka, the eastern Himalayas and the Philippines. These nine areas alone contain almost 22,500 endemic plant species or 45 per cent of the hot-spots' total – and 9 per cent of the planet's total plant species.

Cradles of modern agriculture. Wild genetic resources make a marked contribution to agriculture and the health of the world's harvests. Rice, wheat and maize supply nearly half the world's food, while another four – barley, potato, sweet potato and cassava – bring the total to three quarters. Yet these few food crops are constantly threatened by new diseases and pathogens. To counter the threat, plant breeders must regularly enhance the crops' genetic makeup through infusions of wild germplasm.[139] This cross-breeding keeps commercial crop varieties healthy and more robust.

Maize has been particularly susceptible to diseases. After a blight caused over $2 billion of damage to the maize crop in the United States during the early 1970s, a disease-resistant germplasm was found from non-commercial sources. In the late 1970s, a relative of modern maize was discovered in Mexico, actually in a montane forest that was about to be cleared. Termed "the botanical find of the century", this wild variety offers resistance to no fewer than six major diseases. In addition, it can be grown in areas cooler and wetter than are tolerated by commercial maize, so it opens up the prospect that the range of modern maize could be expanded by a full fifth.[139]

Many other wild varieties of modern crops are available in wildland habitats. Because of habitat destruction, we are losing genetic resources of exceptional value. Yet these "cradles of modern agriculture" are all severely threatened: Mexico, Central America, the Andes of South America, the Ethiopian highlands, the Middle East, and South and Southeast Asia, among other localities. It is imperative that while seeking to protect the planetary stock of plant and animal species, we also conserve areas rich in wild germplasm.

QUALITY OF LIFE

According to UNFPA's 1990 annual report, *The State of World Population*, "the quality of human life is inseparable from the quality of the environment. It is increasingly clear that both are inseparable from the question of human numbers and concentrations. One of the clearest lessons of the last two decades of work in population is that investments in human resource development – for example, improvements in women's status, access to education, health and family planning services – have been seen not only to improve the quality of life, but serve also as the best and quickest way to reduce population growth rates. By opening up options in the present, they open up options for the future."[1]

Another recent United Nations report, *The Human Development Report 1990*,[140] presents an index that measures development in its broadest sense. The criteria are not only income or per capita Gross Domestic Product (GDP), but life expectancy (especially for under-five-year-olds), health, literacy (especially for females), school enrolment, food security, wealth distribution, military expenditures, population growth rates, fertility, contraceptive prevalence and natural resource stocks. It concludes that a significant reduction in population growth rates is absolutely essential for demonstrable improvements in human development levels: "Population growth has outpaced part of development's success."

In this section, nine salient development sectors are assessed in terms of their relationship to population factors.

Health

Particularly important is the question of the welfare of mothers and children. There is a long way to go on both these fronts. In the case of

TWO HEALTH INDICATORS

Region	Life expectancy (years)		Child mortality (deaths per 1,000 children)	
	1950-55	1980-88	1960-65	1980-85
World	49.9	64.6	117	81
Africa	37.5	49.7	157	114
Asia	41.2	57.9	133	87
South America	52.3	64.0	101	64
North America	64.4	71.1	43	27
Europe	65.3	73.2	37	19
Soviet Union	61.7	70.9	32	25
Oceania	61.0	67.6	35	39

children aged five and less, annual mortality in developing countries is still around 13 million deaths a year, many of them environment related.[141,142] The infant mortality rate is 70 per 1,000 births, compared with 12 in developed countries. In the most environmentally degraded region, Africa, it is 94 per 1,000 live births; those African countries most affected by desertification feature the highest percentages of malnutrition. More than 150 million children in developing countries are malnourished, a condition that leaves them all the more vulnerable to diseases that are the immediate cause of mortality.[143,144] In turn, much malnutrition stems from their parents' trying to practise agriculture in overloaded environments and being too impoverished to buy food.[142] Many childhood diseases are due to inadequate supplies of freshwater for household purposes such as drinking, cooking and sanitation; the great bulk of child mortality stems from water-related diseases.

In addition, children suffer unduly from pollution.[145] This is because children have higher metabolic and consumption rates. A child inhales about twice as much air per unit of body weight as does an adult, which puts it at twice the risk from air-borne pollutants. Furthermore, children absorb more pesticides because they eat proportionately more fruit and vegetables that may well have been treated with pesticides.[141]

There is another link-up between child welfare and population planning activities. Poorly spaced births – often due to a lack of family planning services – are a source of much infant mortality. For instance, children born less than two years after the previous child are 66 per cent more likely to die in infancy.[1] More generally, "By preventing... pregnancies that occur too early, too late and too close together, family planning can save millions of children's lives each year... Children born to mothers who are very young, very old, or who recently gave birth are more likely to be born with low birth weight. Children born into large families have to compete with other siblings for food, clothing, and parental attention, and are more susceptible to infection. If these children survive their vulnerable childhood years, their growth is more likely to be stunted, their intellectual development impaired, and their prospects for adult life greatly diminished."[1]

As for women's health, the maternal mortality rate in developing countries is roughly 450 deaths per 100,000 live births (15 times higher than in developed countries), with a total of 500,000 deaths a year.[146-148] At least as many are left with lives permanently and severely impaired because of complications during pregnancy and birth. Non-medical abortions account for 200,000 maternal deaths every year.[8] This blot on the health record of developing countries reflects in part the lack of family planning services; if contraceptives or other forms of birth-control were readily available, there would be far fewer hazardous abortions.[149]

But the high level of maternal mortality also reflects the poor health of developing-country women overall, due particularly to poor diets and frequent illness. In turn, these deficiencies reflect resource constraints and environmental degradation: the lack of sufficient food, clean water, and energy all aggravated by the pressures of too many people.[150] Even more important, developing-world women cannot make their full contribution to sustainable development – in which they play several crucial roles – as long as they remain susceptible to permanent ill-health through being undernourished, over-worked and burdened with almost constant pregnancy.[151,152]

Employment

Employment is likewise related to environmental concerns. If the fast-growing numbers in the workforce of many developing countries cannot find suitable employment, they face three choices: to further overload agricultural lands, to migrate to urban areas that cannot accommodate their present multitudes, or to join the throngs of landless people who migrate to marginal zones, the zones that, being too wet, too dry or too hilly for conventional agriculture, are most susceptible to environmental damage. This last linkage cannot be demonstrated conclusively in causative terms, since it has hardly been researched, let alone documented and analyzed in detail. But the case is apparent with respect to deforestation, if only in qualitative terms, insofar as there is a linkage between rapid population growth, unemployment (plus landlessness), migration to forestlands, and expansion of slash-and-burn farming.[153,154,117,155] There is a putative parallel linkage in connection with desertification;[74] and in the instance of soil erosion,[58] as indicated under the section *Agricultural lands*.

While an expanding workforce can offer a number of benefits for a developing economy,[156] a too rapidly expanding workforce can generate problems in the form of massive unemployment and underemployment in the absence of sufficient socio-economic infrastructure to supply jobs. As of 1990, around 1.8 billion people in the developing world were either working or seeking work;[157] of these, the total unemployed and underemployed exceeded half a billion people (which is almost as many as the entire workforce of the developed world). And because of the sheer increase in human numbers, the 1990 workforce of 1.8 billion is projected to grow to 2.1 billion in 2000 and 3.1 billion in 2025.[158] Every year during the 1990s, developing countries must create an average of 30 million jobs just to prevent the present unemployment and underemployment from growing worse.

Consider the case of Latin America. During the last two decades of this century the region must create jobs equal to 230 per cent of what the United States achieved during the best two decades of its history, yet do it with an economy only one third that of the United States today. Mexico alone must generate a million jobs a year throughout the 1990s just to prevent unemployment and underemployment from growing still more acute. This is half as many jobs as the United States aims to create during the same period, yet Mexico must do it with an economy only a thirtieth the size of the United States'.

An even worse prospect faces sub-Saharan Africa, where

unemployment and underemployment already run at a level of at least 40 per cent.[159] Yet to keep up with the number of potential work seekers already born, the region will have to create an annual total of 6 million jobs during the 1990s, and 10 million throughout the first quarter of next century, merely to keep abreast of the tide of young adults entering the workforce. Yet, it must do this with a combined GDP (South Africa excepted) equivalent to that of Belgium. If the region fails to attain this investment level, there will be a marked increase in poverty, and an even more marked increase in the numbers of absolute poor who will feel obliged to seek their livelihoods in marginal environments.

Landlessness
Closely associated with the lack-of-work issue is the lack-of-land issue. Both reflect an inadequate socio-economic infrastructure and an inadequate natural resource base in face of unprecedented population growth rates. Equally to the point, both issues lead to increasing numbers of marginal people with no apparent alternative but to migrate to marginal environments.

Landlessness, together with near-landlessness (insufficient land to support a farming household), is already a widespread phenomenon in many developing countries.[121,160,161] It is specially pronounced in South and Southeast Asia.[160,162-166] In Bangladesh, almost 50 per cent of rural households were landless or cultivated less than 0.2 of a hectare in 1983; since then the situation has deteriorated sharply because of the pressures of population growth. In Thailand, in 1984, landlessness characterized 10 per cent of rural households, 23 per cent of whom cultivated only 0.8 of a hectare. In the Philippines, 37 per cent of rural households were classified as landless in 1982. Certainly, the situation could be relieved if there were better provision for off-farm employment and other measures to enable landless people to support themselves. But partly because of the gross inadequacy of socio-economic infrastructure, and partly because of the pressures of rapid population growth – the one factor serves to reinforce the other – there is a pronounced and fast-growing problem of destitution on the part of those without sufficient land to support themselves.

While the pressures of population growth and lack of socio-economic infrastructure are not so profound and pervasive in Latin America, they are still acute in a large and growing number of countries.[160,167-170] The result is an increase in the phenomenon of the marginal person in marginal environments.

PROPORTION OF WORLD POPULATION LIVING IN URBAN AREAS

☐ RURAL

■ URBAN

Height of bars indicates
population in billions

WORLD TOTAL

DEVELOPING REGIONS

DEVELOPED REGIONS

AFRICA

EAST ASIA

LATIN AMERICA

SOUTH ASIA

Urbanization

Urbanization has become a dominant trend in the growth and distribution of population. In 1950, only 29 per cent of humankind lived in urban communities, but today, a mere four decades later, the proportion is approaching 50 per cent. By far the greatest part of this urbanization trend is taking place in the developing world. Developing-world city numbers are projected to surge from a total of well under 2 billion people today to almost 4 billion by 2025, by which time the developing world will be almost as urbanized as the developed world.[171-175]

This makes for one of the most extreme demographic phenomena since people started to gather in cities 5,000 years ago. The environment and development repercussions are profound, as urban authorities strive to provide infrastructure and basic services such as housing, energy, water, sewage disposal, transportation and general utilities. The challenge is enormous. Many urban communities are expanding at least twice as fast as national populations.[172,176,177]

The phenomenon is most marked in the largest cities. Worldwide one out of 10 persons now lives in a city of 2 million people or more, most of them in developing countries. Of the 25 largest cities, 19 are in developing countries, which are the least able to tackle problems of urban degradation, industrial pollution, waste generation and general congestion. The largest of all are far beyond all previous human experience of urban living. Mexico City is now crammed with 18 million people, or as many as the national populations of Sweden, Norway and Denmark combined; it is projected to reach almost 25 million in another 10 years time. São Paulo will not be far behind, while Calcutta, Bombay and Shanghai will reach nearly 16 million, and Teheran, Jakarta, Buenos Aires, Rio de Janeiro, Seoul and Delhi are all expected to exceed 12 million people – a total considered until recently to be the limit for even the largest urban conglomerations.

Some exploratory research suggests there could well be a threshold for acceptable size of about a million people.[171] Below this level a city can provide amenities that outweigh the disadvantages of an acute concentration of people; above it, there is a progressive overloading of housing and other services. Yet, the biggest cities attract the most people, even though they are the least capable of meeting basic needs. Much of the low-grade employment growth is drawn into these outsized urban communities, swelling them far beyond their real economic base. Robert McNamara, former President of the World Bank, is sceptical that such huge agglomerations can be made to work at all. "These sizes [of cities] are such that any economies of location

25 LARGEST CITIES AND THEIR PROJECTED POPULATIONS

City	1985 population (millions)	Projected year 2000 population (millions)
Mexico City	17	25
São Paulo	16	24
Tokyo	19	21
New York City	16	16
Calcutta	10	16
Greater Bombay	10	16
Shanghai	12	15
Teheran	7	14
Jakarta	8	13
Buenos Aires	11	13
Rio de Janeiro	10	13
Seoul	10	13
Delhi	7	13
Lagos	6	12
Cairo	8	12
Karachi	6	12
Manila	7	12
Beijing	9	12
Dhaka	5	11
Los Angeles	10	11
London	11	11
Bangkok	6	10
Moscow	9	10
Tianjin	8	10
Osaka	8	10

Note: only six of the 25 cities are in developed countries. In 1950 their aggregate population was 42 million people. By 2000 they will feature an additional 36 million people, an 86 per cent increase. The remaining 19 cities, located in developing countries, had a total 1950 population of 58 million. By 2000, it is projected to expand by an additional 203 million inhabitants (350 per cent).

are dwarfed by costs of congestion. The rapid population growth that has produced them will have far outpaced the growth of human and physical infrastructure needed for even moderately efficient economic life and orderly political and social relationships, let alone amenity for their residents."[178]

Consider, for instance, sheer congestion. In Bangkok, traffic jams are so severe that the amount of passengers' time lost on city streets, plus the amount of extra gasoline consumed, are reckoned to cost at least $1 billion a year. A further $1 billion is lost through medical bills and worker absenteeism because of pollution-related ailments, as well as through damage to buildings and the like.[179] In developing-world cities generally, more than a billion people are believed to be living in conditions so polluted that the air is not fit to breathe.[180]

Worse, most cities in the developing world have become loci for some of the most degrading poverty known, with vast throngs of people living on the margins of survival. Of every 100 new households established in urban areas of developing countries during the second half of the 1980s, 72 were located in shanties and slums (92 out of every 100 in Africa). Today, an estimated 1.2 billion people – almost 23 per cent of all people on Earth, and 60 per cent of Third World city-dwellers – live in squatter settlements, often shantytowns fashioned from cardboard, plastic, canvas or whatever other material is available. These squalid environments are breeding grounds for disease. Yet the number of urban households in the developing world without safe water increased from 138 million in 1970 to 215 million by 1988 (a 56 per cent increase in just 18 years), and those without adequate sanitation rose from 98 million to 340 million, or by 247 per cent.[1,172]

But as in several other sectors described above, population growth and the immigration of impoverished people are not the only factors at work. Misguided policies for urban planning, especially in the form of outmoded building regulations, also contribute to the problem.[172] In Nairobi's slums, simple homes could be upgraded at a cost of only $340 each, but this measure is blocked by the city's by-laws that reflect colonial-era building codes, making it impossible to build an "official" house for less than 10 times as much. The law still requires, for instance, that every dwelling be accessible by car. As a result, the richest tenth of Nairobi's citizens occupy two thirds of the city's residential land; and there are at least 100,000 slum-style houses that cannot be improved by legal means. Similarly in Manila, 88 per cent of the population is too poor to buy or rent an officially "legal" house. In the developing world as a whole, as much as 70 and sometimes 95 per cent of all new urban housing is to some extent "illegal".

Overwhelming as urban problems are, they appear set to grow worse by virtue of the sheer upsurge in human numbers and lack of the most rudimentary facilities. During the 1970s, urban communities had to accommodate another 30 million people each year – a challenge that plainly exceeded the planning capacities of most governments. During the 1990s, the total could well be twice as many and, by 2025, it could even reach 90 million a year. The overall total of developing-world urban populations expanded from a mere 286 million people in 1950 to over 1.5 billion by 1990 (a 526 per cent increase). It is expected to reach 4.4 billion by the year 2025 (another 293 per cent increase over 1990 levels).[1]

Population distribution and migration

The section on *Urbanization* has pointed out the many acute problems generated by population distribution, or rather maldistribution. Simply stated, it is a case of too many people gathering too fast in too few localities with too few resources to support them. Unlike certain of the problems described above, this one is well recognized: it is frequently and emphatically identified by governments as one of the most vital issues on the population front.

During the second half of this century, city dwellers in the developing world will have increased their numbers over seven times. Contrast this with the situation in the developed world where the number of people living in cities has little more than doubled. While many factors are involved, of both "push" and "pull" sorts, a key ingredient is sheer increase in human numbers. In turn, the distributional aspect of population growth has become an important environmental concern. First, as we have just seen under *Urbanization*, there are not enough resources (water, food, energy, etc.) to support the mushrooming multitudes in urban areas. Second, the extreme concentration of human numbers in urban areas generates a knock-on effect with regard to rural environments, insofar as they exert a distinctly parasitic impact on natural resource stocks in their supporting hinterlands.

For instance, cities' energy demands sometimes cause fuelwood supplies to be depleted for a radius of 80 to 150 kilometres.[122,181,182] Delhi imports some of its fuelwood from 1,000 kilometres away in Assam.[183] A study of fuelwood use in Kenya reveals that the major contributor to deforestation is not rural fuelwood use, which is mostly sustainable, but rather the conversion of wood to charcoal for sale to people living in towns and cities. Hence, there is a direct link between energy preferences in urban areas and an environmental crisis that has previously been thought to lie at the doorstep of rural consumers.[15] The World Bank estimates that by the year 2000 the urban areas of West Africa will account for 50 to 70 per cent of the region's fuelwood consumption, at a time when fuelwood stocks will be considerably more depleted than they are today, thus adding to the impoverishment of rural people.[159]

There is every prospect for a continuing over-concentration of developing-world people, including many of the poorest, in urban areas. Maldistribution of population is set to grow steadily worse. Projections indicate that urban communities will expand from 1.5 billion to 2.7 billion people, an 80 per cent increase in just the next 15 years. As early as 2010, when the developing world's rural population is projected to attain 2.8 billion people, the total is expected to stop growing altogether, possibly even going into decline as the city-directed distribution of population continues. Given experience to date, this carries momentous implications for natural resource use and environmental welfare in both urban and rural areas alike. Plainly, there is a premium on better distribution of populations so that they accord with the natural resource stocks needed to support them, primarily in rural areas.

Environmental refugees

There could soon be major population shifts of a different sort resulting from the phenomenon of environmental refugees; these being people obliged to leave their homelands because there is no longer any prospect of their deriving even the most meagre livelihood there.[184,185] The phenomenon derives both from population growth and environmental deterioration, leading to an extreme degree of human deprivation. Trying to assess the eventual numbers of these refugees is a matter of speculation: it is not possible to determine the ultimate scope of the phenomenon. But since it will profoundly affect multitudes of people, a cursory assessment is appropriate.

Already there are at least 10 million of these environmental refugees – more than the total refugees at the end of World War II. To put the problem in perspective, consider a not unlikely outlook for Bangladesh, an England or Florida-sized country with 115 million people today, projected to exceed 200 million by 2020 and 350 million by 2050. If the sea level eventually rises by one metre, as climate change models predict, the ultimate outcome could be catastrophic. Up to 120 million Bangladeshis could be made homeless.[46-48] The victims could look for little help from an already poor nation that would have lost a sizable share of its economic base within the inundated zone.

In the Nile delta too, sea level rise is projected to lead to the elimination of almost a fifth of Egypt's habitable land. The area most under threat already features a population density twice that of Bangladesh. Flooding would be likely to cause the displacement of around 20 million people.[47,48] This scenario, moreover, is cautious and conservative: there would surely be additional problems, such as the intrusion of saltwater up the foreshortened Nile, which would further reduce the irrigated lands that make up virtually the whole of Egypt's agriculture.

Deltas are unusually vulnerable to even a moderate amount of sea level rise. Yet these are precisely the areas that feature some of the densest human settlements and most intensive agriculture on Earth. Among such "severe risk" areas are the estuaries of the rivers Hwang Ho, Yangtze, Mekong, Chao Phraya, Salween, Irrawaddy, Indus, Tigris/Euphrates, Zambezi, Niger, Gambia, Senegal, Courantyne and Maruni (in the Guyanas), and La Plata. Given present populations and their growth rates, at least 100 million people would find themselves flooded out or suffering related troubles from periodic storm surges, coastal erosion, and saltwater intrusion into groundwater aquifers. Furthermore, the newly created coastal zones would be more crowded than ever.[186]

Still other communities could be threatened in low-lying coastal territories, notably the metropolises of Jakarta, Madras, Bombay, Karachi, Lagos and Rio de Janeiro. If only half of their projected populations eventually become displaced, that will add 40 million people to the refugee total. At the same time a number of developed-world cities will be threatened as well, notably Rotterdam, Venice, New York, Miami and New Orleans. But developed nations have the engineering skills and the finances to hold back the sea with massive dikes, after the manner of the Netherlands; or they could go some way toward moving their cities inland. Neither of these options is open to developing nations.

In broader terms, a one-metre rise in sea level would threaten almost 5 million square kilometres of coastal lands in total. While this is roughly equivalent to the United States west of the Mississippi River, it amounts to only 3 per cent of Earth's land surface. Yet it encompasses a full third of global croplands and is home to well over a billion people already, a figure projected to rise to over 2 billion within a few decades. In addition to areas mentioned above, affected coastal zones could generate another 50 million refugees. Today, 30 million Chinese live in coastal lands a mere half metre above sea level.

Then there is the prospect of other greenhouse effects such as continuous droughts and dislocation of monsoon systems. According to a recent study,[38] there could be a 10 per cent reduction in the global grain harvest on average three times a decade; the 1988 droughts that stressed the United States, Canada and China resulted in almost a 5 per cent decline in food output. Given that the world's food reserves have dwindled almost to nothing as a result of the late-1980s' droughts, it is not unrealistic to reckon that each such grain harvest shortfall could result in the starvation deaths of between 50 and 400 million people. Catastrophes of this order would trigger mass migrations of people from famine-affected areas. Although it is not possible to say how many people may be driven from their land by droughts and famine, a best rough estimate puts the total at roughly 50 million refugees.

Wastes and pollution
In this field, the population linkage is not so apparent and dominant as in most of the sectors already analyzed. According to Barry Commoner, "the theory that environmental degradation is largely due to population growth is not supported by the data."[187,188] Rather the responsibility lies, Commoner believes, with negligent technology, especially on the part of industrial countries. Even though these countries contain less than a quarter of the world's population, they were responsible in 1985 for three quarters of the world's 2.5 billion tonnes of waste. Their per capita waste now averages 1.6 tonnes a year, or about 10 times as much as in developing countries.

But according to one incisive analysis, the developed world/developing world share could change drastically.[12] Because of population growth alone, the developing world is projected to contribute 60 per cent of all new waste generated between 1985 and 2025. If we add in the factor of income growth, we find the developing world's share rises to 83 per cent – even though per capita waste would still be only 0.34 tonnes, or little more than a fifth of what a developed-world citizen generates today. Of course, there could be some relief from anti-pollution technologies, but recent experience suggests these may not be so promising as one might suppose.

In a further analysis, this time with respect to pollution from nitrates, cars and electricity in 65 developing countries, Commoner determines that well over half of the problem stems from technologies of production.[187] But population growth is still responsible for between 24 and 31 per cent of the increase in pollution. While this share is much less than that of technology, it is a great deal more than that attributed to changes in consumption levels.[12] Hence, it is important to regard slower population growth as a valuable measure, albeit not the only measure, in curbing pollution.

Poverty
A key component in all these *Quality of Life* issues is absolute poverty, defined by Robert McNamara as "a condition of life so limited by

malnutrition, illiteracy, disease, squalid surroundings, high infant mortality and low life expectancy as to be beneath any reasonable definition of human decency".[178] This profound problem is widespread in developing countries, and it is growing worse.[22,26,189] It reflects questions of both population and environment.

The total number of malnourished people in 1981 was 460 million; in 1987, it was 512 million. Today, 770 million people receive insufficient food for an active working life. One child in six is born underweight, a proportion that rises twice as high by age five. More than 1.3 billion people lack access to safe drinking water. Each year 13 million children – one in 10 of all children born – die of water-related diseases or malnutrition. In many developing countries the 1980s have seen population growth outstripping economic growth. In two thirds of these countries there has been a decline of per capita income, in some instances by as much as 25 per cent.[1,22,26,142,190,191]

In most countries where these adverse circumstances prevail, population growth remains high, and must be reckoned a preeminent factor in the deteriorating situation. As noted in Chapter 1, between 15 and 30 per cent of developing-world families have eight or more members, but among poor families the proportion rises to 55 to 80 per cent.[26,192] Thus, population growth is fastest among the poorest countries. Southern Asia, with almost 23 per cent of the world's present population, is projected to account for 31 per cent of population increase during the 1990s. In Africa, the figures are 12 per cent and 23 per cent, respectively. Yet the poorest people are the ones least able to cope with the needs of fast-growing numbers, and the poorest countries find the inadequacy of their development efforts is reinforced by the rapid buildup of still more impoverished people who, by their sheer numbers, overwhelm socio-economic infrastructure.

A second determinant of poverty is environmental decline. The bottom billion are unusually dependent on their environmental resource base – soils, vegetation and water that constitute their main stocks of economic capital. At the same time, impoverished communities feel impelled, by force of circumstances, to over-exploit their environmental resource base. They perceive no alternative to misusing and over-using these resource stocks today even at cost to their livelihood tomorrow. So they are driven to deplete their main means of future survival. In turn, this serves to entrench their poverty, and appears to foster the motivation for large families. The bottom billion face an outlook of ever greater constraints.

As a further measure of the impoverished plight of those countries featuring the bottom billion, their cereal food imports in 1970 totalled only 20 million tonnes but, by 1984, they were importing 69 million tonnes. The import total is projected to increase to 112 million tonnes by the year 2000.[191,193,194]

A salient aspect of this whole issue is the "feminization of poverty".[192] The impoverished are rather more likely to be female than male, particularly in urban areas. Life in general is harsher for poor women than poor men. This raises the whole question of the status of women and what can be done to improve it.

Women's status

Most of the sectors examined under *Quality of Life* are particularly relevant to developing-world women who suffer unduly from deficiencies in infrastructural systems for health, education, employment and agriculture. This reflects women's standing as distinctly second-class citizens, despite international initiatives such as the United Nations Convention on The Elimination of All Forms of Discrimination Against Women – a measure ratified by more than 120 governments, but still disregarded in much of the world. Of course, women should be able to enjoy their full share of development benefits as a simple matter of equity. But their disadvantaged status is all the more regrettable in that they play a central role in all development activities and particularly in the population sphere; and they play a significant, albeit little recognized, role as *de facto* environmental managers. Because of these multiple roles, women's activities are crucial to sustainable development.[151,152,195-201]

With particular respect to environmental concerns, women's efforts to gain their families' livelihoods mean they are often more closely involved with natural resource stocks (soil, water, forests) as well as with the management of water, sanitation and domestic waste, than are men. In several parts of sub-Saharan Africa, women are responsible for up to 70 per cent of the production, processing and marketing of food, with all it entails in terms of the environmental resource base that underpins agriculture. In Kenya, they are the principal participants in the National Soil Conservation Programme which has resulted in the terracing of more than 360,000 farms, or 40 per cent of the nation's total.[18]

In many areas of the developing world, women traditionally endure the added burden of gathering fuelwood, and they often have the lead in tree planting. In areas where there are severe fuelwood deficits, women spend five to 10 hours several times a week walking long distances to find fuelwood for their fires and fodder for their

Nepal: building a better future

Nepal is one of the poorest countries in the world, with an average per capita income of $180 a year. The country's 19.5 million people are largely rural. Many of them eke out a subsistence living on hilly land given to extremes of weather: exceptional heat in the dry season, monsoonal rains during the wet months. Most rural communities lack basic sanitation facilities or access to clean water. Only the larger towns have electricity; many mountain villages still obtain most of their energy needs from fuelwood or crop residues.

In the village of Chautara, situated in the hills east of Kathmandu, the Family Planning Association of Nepal, in cooperation with World Neighbors, has launched a highly successful integrated development project – one of the largest in the country. Called the Boudha Bahunepati Family Welfare Project, it includes 20,000 households with around 130,000 people.

"We cannot introduce successful family planning without first raising the income level of the villagers in this region," points out Pradash Bahadur Kayastha, programme officer at the Family Welfare Centre in Chautara. "Most people here live on the edge of survival. So we are concentrating our efforts first on the provision of basic services such as clean water, sanitation (pit latrines), and primary health care, coupled to erosion control and the planting of fuelwood and fodder trees. We also distribute vegetable seeds for kitchen gardens and fruit trees as a way of giving villagers more ways to earn some cash income."

Behind the success of the project is the determination of the region's women to improve their lives. One woman in particular has been a catalyst in stimulating change; in getting village women to play their full role in development. Mrs. Shanti Basnet is the local village health motivator for Chautara and nearby villages, a job she has held for 11 years. She confesses that, at first, it was not easy to coax families into accepting the necessity for planning families. "I tell people that so long as you can support your children, have them. But the problem is, so many people cannot adequately support the children they do have. But we cannot preach family planning outside the context of village development. Only when family planning is connected to development issues do we win the confidence of the people."

Shanti Basnet has certainly made a difference in Chautara. Her success in promoting family planning and basic health care is impressive. On average, 32 per cent of the women of child-bearing age in the region practise family planning – a rate nearly double the national average of 19 per cent.

A great part of Shanti's success is due to her low-key indirect approach to family planning in an area where basic survival is a day-to-day struggle. Although family planning and better health care were prime objectives, they were not included until more basic development goals had been achieved – the provision of clean water, sanitary latrines and above all income-generating activities for the poorest segments of society.

Today, women attend literacy classes, tend vegetable and fruit gardens in order to earn extra income and practise family planning. As a result, population growth rates are down to 1.4 per cent a year for the villages of Bahunepati, Chautara and nearby Maguwa. Women also participate in soil erosion control programmes and other local conservation activities.

In an area that used to be one of the poorest in the entire country, the Bahunepati region is now on its way to recovery, thanks in large measure to women like Shanti Basnet.

animals.[202] In Burkina Faso, women from the village of Kalsaka spend four hours several times a week in seeking fuelwood. Stocks nearer to home have been depleted.[202] In parts of Nepal, they now have to hike so far they must assign an extra hour each day for the purpose – with the result that their on-farm activities suffer appreciably.[129]

At the same time, women are often denied the opportunity to contribute to sustainable development because they are over-burdened with bearing and rearing children. Their status within the community tends to be defined by their capacity to produce large families, generally larger than they can cope with. Their lack of education and job security, together with their poor status generally, means there is pressure for women to marry early which further promotes high fertility, especially in countries where family income is supported by children's labour.

To resolve the problem, there is an urgent need to:
• Improve women's status through fundamental social and political changes that give women more freedom in all decisions that affect their lives: delaying the age at which they marry, allowing women to inherit property and giving them voting rights, among other things.
• Ensure that family planning services are readily available.
• Enhance women's motivation in favour of smaller families through increased access to better maternal and child health care.
• Prolong female enrolments in school. Education, in particular, can have a dramatic effect on fertility levels. Extending the period girls remain in school from an average of three years to between four and

six results in a reduction of fertility rates of 5 per cent in Asia and Africa and 15 per cent in Latin America. Improved educational opportunities also translate into better sanitary conditions at home and healthier families.

• Provide women with far better employment opportunities. Women who work are able to contribute more substantially to their families' welfare by increasing their status within society. They also tend to be more motivated to adopt family planning and to space births appropriately.

It is only through the full and equal participation in society, at all levels, that women will be able to realize their full potential.[152,199,203] Above all, these measures are valid in their own right and should be provided on basic humanitarian grounds.

CHAPTER 3

POPULATION CARRYING CAPACITIES:
SEVEN CASE STUDIES

The population-environment linkages cited thus far are well illustrated by the experience of a number of individual countries as will now be documented. These case study assessments serve to point up a cross-cutting factor that is central to population concerns – the concept of population carrying capacity.

THE CONCEPT OF POPULATION CARRYING CAPACITY

Population carrying capacity is a critical and controversial issue. Certain observers (often ecologists) tend to assert that it is not only a key constraint to population growth, but that it can readily become an absolute factor. Other observers (often economists) tend to assert that carrying capacity is such a flexible affair, subject to endless expansion through technology and policy interventions, that it soon ceases to have much operational value at all.

Population carrying capacity can be defined as "the number of people that the planet can support without irreversibly reducing its capacity or ability to support people in the future."[25,204-206] While this is a global-level definition, it applies at national level too, albeit with many qualifications, for example, international trade, investment and debt. Furthermore, it is a function of factors that reflect technological change, food and energy supplies, ecosystem services (such as provision of freshwater and recycling of nutrients), human capital, people's lifestyles, social institutions, political structures and cultural constraints among many other factors, all of which interact with each other.

Two points are particularly important: that carrying capacity is ultimately determined by the component that yields the lowest carrying capacity; and that human communities must learn to live off the "interest" of environmental resources rather than off their "principal".[204] Thus, the concept of carrying capacity is closely tied in with the concept of sustainable development. There is now evidence that human numbers with their consumption of resources, plus the technologies deployed to supply that consumption, are often exceeding the land's carrying capacity already. In many parts of the world, the three principal and essential stocks of renewable resources – forests, grasslands and fisheries – are being utilized faster than their

71

rate of natural replenishment.[93]

Consider a specific example – the Earth's carrying capacity with respect to food production. According to the World Hunger Project,[191] the planetary ecosystem could, with present agro-technologies and with equal distribution of food supplies, satisfactorily support 5.5 billion people if they all lived on a vegetarian diet (the 1991 global population is already 5.4 billion). If people derived 15 per cent of their calories from animal products, as tends to be the case in South America, the total would decline to 3.7 billion. If they derived 25 per cent of their calories from animal protein, as is the case with most people in North America, the Earth could support only 2.8 billion people.

True, these calculations reflect no more than today's food-production technologies. Certain observers protest that such an analysis underestimates the scope for technological expertise to keep on expanding the Earth's carrying capacity.[207] We can surely hope that many advances in agro-technologies will come on stream. But consider the population-food record over the past four decades. From 1950 to 1984, and thanks largely to remarkable advances in Green Revolution agriculture, there was a 2.6-fold increase in world grain output. This achievement, representing an average increase of almost 3 per cent a year, raised per capita production by more than a third. But from 1985 to 1989, there was next to no increase at all, even though the period saw the world's farmers investing billions of dollars to increase output (fertilizer use alone expanded by 14 per cent). These big investments were supported by rising grain prices and by the restoration to production of idled United States cropland. Crop yields had "plateaued"; it appeared that plant breeders and agronomists had exhausted the scope for technological innovation. So the 1989 harvest was hardly any higher than that of 1984. During that same period, there were an extra 440 million people to feed. While world population increased by almost 8.5 per cent, grain output per person declined by nearly 7 per cent.[5, 208]

To put the case more succinctly, every 15 seconds sees the arrival of another 44 people, and during the same 15 seconds the planet's stock of arable land declines by one hectare.[5] Plainly, this is not to say the first is a singularly causative factor of the second. Many other factors, notably technology, contribute to the linkage. Equally, it is not to deny that there is a strong relationship between the two factors: more people are trying to sustain themselves from less cropland.

Regrettably, there is all too little concise analysis of the concept of carrying capacity. So the evaluation of its nature, and especially of the threat of environmental overloading, must remain largely a matter of judgment. But remember that in a situation of pervasive uncertainty, we have no alternative but to aim for the best assessment we can muster. We cannot defer the question until such time as we have conducted enough research. After all, if we do not derive such conclusions as we can and make explicit planning decisions on their basis, there will be implicit planning decisions taken by large numbers of people who, through their daily lifestyles, are determining the outcome. In other words, decisions on the population-environment nexus will be taken either by design or by default. We must make do with such information and understanding as we have at hand, however imperfect that may be.

To comprehend the concept of carrying capacity in real-world terms, consider the following case studies. Through the experience of seven countries, drawn from all three main developing regions, we can discern the strong links between population pressure and the capacity of the natural resource base to support increasing human numbers.

PAKISTAN

Pakistan, like its neighbour India, suffers much environmental degradation in the form of deforestation, soil erosion, desertification and depletion of water supplies. This resource decline is leading to agricultural problems; indeed, to a growing incapacity of natural environments to support present human numbers.[209] Yet the country's natural resource base is central to the national economy, with agriculture the largest single development sector. In 1985, agriculture accounted for 32 per cent of Pakistan's GDP, employed 55 per cent of the population and earned 79 per cent of all export revenues.[210]

Pakistan's land area of 887,722 square kilometres is mostly semi-arid or arid.[211-213] At the time of independence in 1947, the populace totalled 31 million people, and the country was self-sufficient in most staple foods. By 1990, the populace totalled 123 million people, and was growing at an annual rate of 2.9 per cent, doubling the population in 24 years. Allowing for a further decline in the death rate and some decline in the birth rate, the population is projected to reach 162 million people by 2000 and 248 million by 2020; more than twice as many people in a mere three decades. But it is questionable whether there will be much fertility decline in the foreseeable future. The average family size today is 7 children (technically expressed as 6.7), the highest in southern Asia except for Afghanistan. This is considered to be due, in part, to the poor social status of women, and the general neglect of women's development needs in this predominately Muslim country.[214] Only 3 per cent of women are educated, and the female to male school enrolment ratio is among the 10 lowest in the world.[215]

Between 1947 and 1985, Pakistan's birth rate fell from 45 to only 43 per 1,000 people. But in 1990, it is estimated to have risen to 44 per 1,000. By contrast, the crude death rate has fallen from over 25 to 13 per 1,000 people, still higher than the rate for India (11 per 1,000) and the average for the region (12 per 1,000). Obviously, there is some scope for a further decline in the death rate. The level of contraceptive use among reproductive-age women is only 8 per cent, one seventh that recorded for the region. So the population size in 2000 and 2020 could be rather higher than projected. With only a marginal decline in the birth rate and a continuing decline in the death rate, Pakistan could find itself trying to support twice as many people in less than a generation, and more than 400 million by the time it has enjoyed another 45 years of nationhood.

The 3.7 times increase in human numbers since 1947 has been accommodated mainly by three major advances in agriculture during the 1960s. These were: the Indus Basin Treaty that provided a greater volume of riverwater for irrigation; a sharp increase in the number of tubewells supplying access to more underground water; and the introduction of high-yielding varieties of grain. Today, there appears to be little opportunity to gain much more advantage from the first two, while the third provided scant support during the 1980s when grain yields plateaued.

Meantime, the country's natural resource base has experienced growing stress for at least 30 years. Consider three key sectors: forestry, water and agricultural land. A maximum of 3 per cent of national territory is still forested, whereas the government believes it should be at least 15 per cent.[216-218] The Director-General of the Pakistan Forestry Institute, referring to deforested watersheds, concludes the country "already faces a grave situation insofar as water for irrigation and power generation is concerned."[219] Yet deforestation seems set to grow worse if only because of growing demand for fuelwood, which in the mid-1980s accounted for 50 per cent of the country's energy requirements and almost 90 per cent of total wood consumption.[220] There was an acute shortage of fuelwood as far back as 1978, when the annual growth of wood was supplying only 62 per cent of the annual harvest.[221,222] Yet demand for fuelwood is projected to double during the last two decades of this century. So there appears to be little relief for watershed forests in the foreseeable future.

Second, water is in short supply, especially for agriculture. An irrigation network covers almost a fifth of the country, the largest such system in the world. Some 156,000 square kilometres of croplands are irrigated, a full 70 per cent of the cropland expanse; a proportion way ahead of Japan's 63 per cent, China's 48 per cent and India's 33 per cent.[223] These irrigated croplands produce 80 per cent of the country's food. Irrigated wheatlands, comprising 38 per cent of all irrigated croplands, and four times as large an area as rainfed wheatlands, average over 2,000 kilograms of harvest per hectare a year, rainfed wheatlands only around 850 kilograms.[211]

But water is the scarcest input to agriculture, and supplies are likely to run out well before other resources such as land, energy, high-yielding grains, fertilizers and pesticides. On four occasions during the 1980s, Pakistan has experienced critical water shortages, leading to inadequate irrigation-water flows for the main crop-growing season. According to the Director of the Pakistan Water and Power Development Authority, "Water supplies presently available for irrigation are already short of optimum crop water requirements... Even if all surface supplies and groundwater reservoirs are exploited, water would still fall far short of future requirements."[224]

Indeed, there is little prospect of increasing the water supply at all. The Indus River and its tributaries could provide perhaps another 25 to 30 per cent in volume, but this would lead to saltwater intrusions into the river's lower reaches.[225-227] Nor is there much scope for recycling irrigation water. Recycled flows are usually only half as useful as original withdrawals, because of grossly declining quality as irrigation channels pick up fertilizers, salts, pesticides and toxic elements from croplands.[216]

Fortunately, there could be much greater efficiency in water use. If water use were better regulated and controlled, the expanse of double-cropped lands could theoretically be tripled.[228] But because of incorrect pricing policies for water, among other factors, wheat yields per hectare/metre (the amount of water needed to cover one hectare to a depth of one metre) have increased from 2.17 tonnes per hectare a year in 1971-76 to only 2.34 tonnes in the period 1981-86, despite the use of improved seeds and expanded use of fertilizers.[225] In addition, there is widespread leakage of irrigation water: the first 20 per cent is lost from conveyance systems, and 40 per cent of the remainder from on-farm water courses, with a further 25 per cent attrition from runoff due to inefficient application to crops (fields are often far from level). Because of policy constraints – perverse water pricing has persisted for two decades – there seems little hope that efficiency of water use will be improved within the foreseeable future.

Associated with problems of water supply is the phenomenon of salinization. At least 24 per cent of Pakistan's croplands are salinized on the surface, and another 29 per cent feature below-surface salinization. Together with waterlogging and alkalization, this means that more than 70 per cent of the country's croplands are affected by water-related degradation.[229]

As a result of these constraints on the agricultural resource base, in conjunction with the pressures of population growth, there is pervasive land hunger. To sustain a subsistence income through agriculture (consistent with nutritional needs of 2,400 calories per adult per day), an average-size family of 7 persons needed 2.5 hectares of farmland in 1980. But even a decade ago, when the population was 30 per cent smaller than today's, two thirds of farm households did not have enough land to support themselves through this means alone.[230] Whereas the amount of cultivated land per rural inhabitant was a third of a hectare in 1983 (already less than the 0.37 of a hectare considered a minimum with agro-technologies available), it is projected to fall to 0.14 of a hectare in the year 2010.[216] Not surprisingly, there is great and growing pressure from agricultural encroachment on the remaining forests. This, in turn, means that deforestation further aggravates water supply problems for downstream agriculture, reducing the carrying capacity of existing farmlands.

This latter phenomenon of positive feedback between factors of environment and development is paralleled by a reinforcing process between environment and population. Deforestation-derived water deficits affect not only agriculture but public health. Water of sufficient quantity and quality is available to only 23 per cent of the rural population. As a result, there is a pervasive problem of water-related diseases, especially among young children: infant mortality remains a good deal higher than in adjoining states of India.[212]

All this is not to deny Pakistan's remarkable achievement in agriculture. During much of its 43 years of nationhood, Pakistan has been self-sufficient in most major food staples. But by reason of population growth alone, the 1988 level of wheat demand – 16 million tonnes – is projected to reach 25 million tonnes by 2000 and 40 million tonnes by 2010; import requirements are projected to grow to 2 million tonnes and 5 million tonnes by each date, respectively. These wheat imports, plus imports of edible oil, are projected to cost 37 billion rupees by 2010 (at 1980 prices), exceeding the value of all projected exports in that year by 25 per cent.[231]

On a more positive side, there is much room to step up agricultural productivity. Farmers achieve only 25 to 30 per cent of demonstrated potential crop yields. Wheat output per hectare is only 85 per cent that of India, corn output 47 per cent that of Turkey, and rice output 46 per cent that of Egypt. And while the expanse of croplands can scarcely be increased any more because of soil and climate factors, some 100,000 square kilometres of wastelands, or rather wasted lands, could, through careful management, be brought into production for raising livestock. So theoretically, Pakistan eventually could feed at least three times as many people, or almost 350 million. How, then, does this leave the concept of population carrying capacity?

In Pakistan's case, it appears to reflect three key factors. First, for the country to achieve much advance at all beyond its present meagre levels of human welfare (GNP per head $350, with little improvement during the 1980s), it is going to have to tackle the challenge of doing most things right most of the time. In other words, it is going to have to do much better with several leading sectors of development – forestry, agriculture, water, public health and population, to name the more relevant – whether through policy reform, improved planning and programming, institutional adaptation, or more advanced and appropriate technology. This "leap ahead" in socio-economic infrastructure has apparently proved beyond the capacities of the government in a situation of growing constraints and stresses on several fronts. Indeed, the challenge would tax the capacities of a nation with vastly more planning experience and with much more extensive infrastructure.

Secondly, and insofar as carrying capacity must be considered a long-term affair, it is questionable whether Pakistan's development record during its four decades of nationhood has been of a sort to prove sustainable into the foreseeable future. There is much evidence that increases in agricultural output have been accomplished at a cost to sustainable productivity, as evidenced by the rundown of the agricultural resource base via land degradation (salinization, soil erosion) and depletion of resource stocks (forests, surface and groundwater reserves). Technology, in the form of high-yielding grains, fertilizers and pesticides, has enabled food production to keep pace with, or even exceed, population growth for most of the last four decades – a remarkable accomplishment by any standard. But there are signs that the "techno-fix" response to growing human numbers, with their growing aspirations, can no longer maintain its momentum.

The third key factor is that whatever opportunity remains for the nation's carrying capacity to keep on expanding through enhanced agricultural output (sorely limited as this is now turning out to be), it would be taxed in the extreme to keep abreast of population growth at a level of 3 per cent a year. Even the most advanced nation would find it difficult to deploy the planning abilities to keep up with a growth rate of that magnitude.

These three factors are crucial to the concept of population carrying capacity for Pakistan. It is difficult to ascertain their individual importance in a conclusive manner, because they have yet to be analyzed (whether in isolation or in combination) to a degree that allows each to be appraised apart from other variables. Nor would a factor-by-factor assessment present the full picture since each interacts with the others in multiple dynamic ways. It may eventually be possible through refined analysis to determine the precise significance of each; to separate out and quantify the carrying-capacity impacts of each, plus their synergistic reinforcing of the other two. Unfortunately, no such analysis has been undertaken.

An operational evaluation of Pakistan's carrying capacity becomes, in essence, a matter of judgment. This judgment should be based upon an informed and considered appraisal of all component factors at issue, together with an assessment of how far the country's problems can be relieved through improved technology, policy changes, institutional innovation and the like in the future. Of course, the future is unknown. But one can usefully speculate in light of the recent past: Pakistan's record during the 1980s surely serves to give warning rather than to inspire hope. Nonetheless, the assessment must remain a matter of judgment – no more and no less.

So while the concept of carrying capacity can still be viewed as something that is putatively expandable in Pakistan's case, there is much evidence to suppose it is practically close to its apparent limits for the foreseeable future – if, indeed, it has not been surpassed already. In these circumstances, it would make sense for Pakistan to respond through two prime strategies: an unprecedented effort to reform agricultural policies together with whatever other measures are necessary to increase food output and to reduce the rate of population growth.

What are the possibilities for population planning? Taking a rather extreme view, were fertility rates to remain constant between 1990 and 2025, total population would grow from approximately 124 million in 1990 to 486 million by 2025. Conversely, were fertility rates to decline to correspond to the United Nations "medium variant" growth projection, total population would rise much less – from approximately 123 million in 1990 to 267 million by 2025. The corresponding reduction in fertility rates to achieve this decline in total population would require bringing the present birth rate down from 47 births per 1,000 population in 1985-90, to 20 births per 1,000 by 2020-25.

Fortunately, Pakistan's present demographic trends are not only a matter of deep national concern, but are mobilizing effective action. Since the 1974 United Nations World Population Conference, the government has consistently viewed its rates of population growth as being "too high" and has sought to support family planning and other population programmes to reduce growth. In addition, the government has consistently viewed its spatial distribution patterns as inappropriate and has sought to decelerate rates of rural-urban migration and to promote a more balanced relationship between population and natural resources.

Balancing resources and human requirements has become a high priority in government planning during the last two five-year national development plans. To achieve its objectives, the government has adopted a population welfare programme which utilizes a multi-sectoral approach with the specific aim of changing desired family size. This approach encourages active participation of governmental and non-governmental organizations, in conjunction with local communities, and aims at strengthening communication strategies. The government's commitment is reflected in a recent statement by the Minister of Planning and Development that "investment in family planning is a crucial investment for a nation. That is why our population welfare programme must rank – and it does – as the top priority in development planning."

A major aim of Pakistan's population welfare programme has been to bring about an increase in the small proportion of married women who knew of any contraceptive method in 1984.[232] Only 20 per cent of currently married women today know of a source of family planning information or supplies, and only 12 per cent have ever used contraception. These figures contrast sharply with Bangladesh where almost 100 per cent of married women knew of some contraceptive method in 1985, and 32 per cent had used some form of contraception.

Clearly, what is required is the financial and human resources to strengthen and consolidate the existing family welfare programme of Pakistan in order to support and expand reproductive health and clinical services; to pursue an integrated clinical training programme for family planning and health personnel; to foster community-based maternal and child health/family planning (MCH/FP) services through family welfare centres; and to expand family planning service delivery through the involvement of traditional medical practitioners (hakeems). It also requires the development of research and evaluation capabilities as regards interrelationships between population, environment and sustainable development; the building up of national capacities in policy analysis; the integration of population factors into national development plans; assistance to promote training of nationals to assure self-reliance in population planning in the future; and strategies to promote extensive population education in the formal and non-formal schooling sector, among workers in urban industry, and among male and female workers in farm settings and rural cooperatives.[233]

INDIA

India features the second largest population on Earth, 853 million people in 1990. With a population growth rate of 2.1 per cent in 1990, and little fertility decline in recent years, the total is projected to reach slightly more than a billion in the year 2000 and 1.4 billion by 2020, assuming the United Nations "medium variant" projection. If, however, fertility rates were to remain constant, India could end up with a staggering 2.1 billion people by the year 2100. Yet there are many signs the country has already exceeded its carrying capacity, if only through its flagging efforts to feed vast numbers of people.[209]

As in the case of Pakistan, a good part of India's economy depends on its natural resource base. India's territory comprises 3.29 million square kilometres, of which 1.43 million square kilometres (43 per cent) are cultivated, and of these some 470,000 square kilometres (33 per cent) are irrigated. It is the irrigated lands that have underpinned India's success in turning itself from a food-deficit nation into a nation with a slight food surplus. But outside the irrigated areas there has been virtually no Green Revolution.[234] The remaining farmlands are rainfed, featuring ultra-low levels of productivity. It is in these lands that most of India's impoverished people live.

Irrigation-water supplies are critically dependent on forested catchments, notably in the Himalayan foothills.[235,236] Yet, according to the National Remote Sensing Agency of India, forest cover declined from nearly 17 per cent of national territory in 1970 to just over 14 per cent in 1981. The government believes forest cover should be 25 per cent of the land area.[237] According to the late Prime Minister Rajiv Gandhi, deforestation has brought the nation "face to face with a major ecological and socio-economic crisis." Yet, despite the important links between forest cover and irrigated agriculture, investment in forestry and soil conservation programmes under the sixth five-year plan has been only 17.9 per cent of investment in large-scale irrigation projects. The late Prime Minister Gandhi called for 48,000 square kilometres to be reforested each year, but only one third of this goal has been achieved to date.

Much of the deforestation is due to excessive fuelwood gathering as well as agricultural encroachment. In 1982, fuelwood demand was estimated at 133 million tonnes, whereas remaining forestlands could sustain an annual harvest of only 39 million tonnes.[238] The gap of 94 million tonnes was ostensibly met either by over-cutting (thus compromising future forest production) or by burning cow dung and crop residues (which compromises future soil fertility). By the end of this century, the gap will be much larger if India's population continues to grow and its forests continue to contract. Indeed, even if all planned plantations are established, there will be a predicted shortfall of 182 million tonnes of wood, or double the shortfall in 1982.[238]

Deforestation has already disrupted India's watershed systems, causing increased downstream flooding during the monsoon and water shortages during the dry season.[239-241] In the Ganges River system, dry season water-flows declined by almost a fifth during the 1970s.[242] Much of India's success in attaining food self-sufficiency by the early 1980s has been due to a doubling of its irrigated area since 1960. Yet because of the degradation of watersheds and the disruption of major water-flows, coupled with a surging demand for municipal and industrial water – partly reflecting the sheer rise in human numbers – India faces the prospect of acute water shortages over much of its territory by the middle of this decade.[238]

Moreover, in 1984, the amount of flood-prone lands nationwide totalled 590,000 square kilometres, compared to only 230,000 square kilometres in 1970.[243] In the Ganges Plains alone, flooding annually affects an area averaging 80,000 square kilometres, including 35,000 square kilometres of valuable croplands.[244] The value of crops lost averages more than $250 million a year, while damage to buildings and public utilities averages around $750 million a year.[245]

On top of this is the problem of land degradation. Some 1.75 million square kilometres are losing agricultural productivity through soil erosion, salinization and waterlogging, with a marked decline in soil fertility and crop yields across an area of a million square kilometres.[60] Soil erosion alone causes Indian farmlands to lose 6 million tonnes a year of nitrogen, phosphorus and potash. Replacing these critical nutrients through chemical fertilizers requires an annual outlay of around $6 billion.[246] In addition, 130,000 square kilometres of irrigated lands suffer from salinization and waterlogging. Much of this land may eventually have to be taken out of production.[247] Land degradation of all sorts is estimated to cause a loss of 30 to 50 million tonnes of produce every year.[248]

In addition, there is the growing problem of siltation. Twenty eight of the biggest irrigation projects have a total catchment area of 690,000 square kilometres, of which 220,000 square kilometres are critically eroded and fewer than 20,000 square kilometres have been rehabilitated.[238] In 1980, 12 irrigation reservoirs were filling with sediment at between two and five times the initial rates, and a good number of others at between six and 20 times the initial rates.[248,249] If only 20 per cent of the live-storage capacity of major and medium-sized reservoirs is silted up by the end of this century, it will mean a loss of irrigation potential equivalent to about 40,000 square kilometres, a full tenth of the present irrigated area.[247] Whereas irrigated lands were meeting the needs of 56 per cent of India's population in 1975, it is planned they will have to meet the needs of 87 per cent of the projected population in the year 2000.[250,251]

All this is not to discount India's remarkable feat in increasing its wheat production from 10 million tonnes in 1964 to more than 45 million tonnes in 1985, and in raising total food grain production to a record 150 million tonnes in 1984.[252,253] For almost a quarter of a century the nation has maintained a sufficient rate of growth in food output to keep just ahead of population growth (though with hardly any increase in per capita food output, and a slight decline in average consumption of calories, protein and fat).[234,254] By the end of the century, however, the nation will need at least 230 million tonnes of food grain each year to feed its growing population, a 53 per cent increase over the 1984 output.[247] These needs notwithstanding, there has been a steady decline in the growth rate of agricultural production since 1960 and, since 1984, there has been virtually no increase at all in food-grain output.

The 1960 to 1984 upsurge in total food production was accomplished primarily in irrigated areas such as those of the Punjab and Haryana States with their level terrain. Additional lands for irrigated agriculture are limited. Not only are watershed supplies of irrigation water becoming irregular, but groundwater stocks have been over-exploited to such an extent that in many areas water tables have dropped by at least one metre. So severe are these water problems that India's future irrigation potential is severely constrained. By 1996, India's food-grain production could well plateau, with per capita output holding at around 204 kilograms, only marginally more than the 195 kilograms of 1985.[238,255] Thereafter, the growth rate for food-grain production could decrease to only 1.9 per cent a year during the period 1996 to 2005, only fractionally higher than the projected growth rate for population. There remains much scope to intensify agricultural production.[252] India has about 20 per cent more land under paddy rice than China, yet produces 40 per cent less. This anomaly is due primarily to the fact that the agricultural resource base is being progressively depleted through land degradation on several fronts.

Thus, profound questions arise about India's capacity to keep feeding its populace which is projected to expand by 190 million, or an additional 22 per cent, by the end of the century. Moreover, the challenge is not only to feed extra people, but also to upgrade nutritional levels among the third of the populace that remains malnourished. If these food-deficient people were to be adequately fed through more efficient and equitable grain distribution, India's grain surplus would be instantly eliminated.

Overall, then, it appears that in certain respects India's renowned Green Revolution has been a short-term success accompanied by long-term costs. India's farmers have posted some impressive results since 1964. But in major measure these advances have been achieved through over-working croplands and over-pumping water stocks. So a key question arises: have Indians been feeding themselves today by borrowing against future food productivity?

Recent trends suggest the outlook is not promising. The annual growth rate in agricultural production in India slipped from an average of 2.8 per cent during 1965-75 to 2.2 per cent during 1981-85, scarcely above the annual rate for population growth. True, there is some scope for India to purchase food from outside sources. But this depends largely on the strength of its economy, burdened as it is with a foreign debt that totalled $37.3 billion in 1987. While this sum appears slight compared with those of certain Latin America nations, debt servicing nevertheless absorbed nearly 19 per cent of India's export earnings.

Furthermore, population growth not only means extra mouths to feed. It exacerbates the problem of landlessness.[121,255,256] The total number of landless households was 15 million in 1961, rising to 26 million by 1981, and is projected to reach 44 million by the year 2000. As noted, agriculture accounts for 79 per cent of employment nationwide. The total workforce is projected to expand from 224 million in 1980 to 376 million in the year 2000, and the level of unemployment and underemployment is not expected to change from its present level of 33 per cent. For off-farm employment to absorb all those who are unemployed and underemployed, non-agricultural sectors would have to grow at more than 12 per cent a year, or well over twice the rate during the decade 1975-84.[255] So there is the prospect of a fast-growing pool of rural people without land or adequately remunerative work.

To reiterate a basic point, these food-population issues place a premium on India's continuing access to water in sufficient amounts at appropriate times of the year. While there is often too much water during the monsoon season, there is often too little during the subsequent dry season. According to a number of reports and analyses summarized in *The State of India's Environment, 1984-1985*,[254] several parts of India could face severe seasonal water deficits by the turn of the century when irrigation demand is projected to be half as high again as it is today and industry's demand to be at least twice as high. This raises the prospect of strife and conflict over water supplies.

Resource-sharing conflicts over the waters of the Ganges River are also a reality. Rising in Nepal, where watershed degradation is pervasive and pronounced, the river runs for 2,700 kilometres before reaching the Bay of Bengal in the Bangladesh delta. Within its valleylands live more than 500 million Indian and Bangladeshi farmers. Bangladesh, occupying the lower reaches of the Ganges River, makes ever greater demands on the river's flows – and the present deteriorating situation arises from a river basin that is projected to feature almost 200 million more people by the end of the century.

Overall hangs the prospect of climatic change, with potentially critical impacts.[257] As we have seen in Chapter 2, a planetary warming is surely on its way, caused by a buildup of carbon dioxide and other greenhouse gases in the atmosphere. As a result of global warming, monsoon systems may be disrupted which could prove critical insofar as India receives 70 per cent of its precipitation from the monsoon. Global warming could also bring on a greater incidence of typhoons and coastal storms along India's coastline, possibly 40 to 50 per cent more destructive than today's due to the increased temperature of the ocean surface.[258-260]

The other side of the carrying capacity equation is population growth. As noted previously, if population growth were to follow the path of the United Nations "constant fertility variant", it will grow from approximately 856 million in 1990 to more than 2 billion by 2025 (implying a constant crude birth rate of about 32 per 1,000 population). Achieving the United Nations "medium variant" projection would result in considerably lower population growth, amounting to about 1.4 billion in 2025; and with the "low variant", an even lower population of 1.3 billion. Achieving the "low variant" would require a drop in crude birth rates from 32 per 1,000 in 1990 to about 13 per 1,000 by 2025.

The government of India has recognized population growth rates as "too high" since the 1974 United Nations Conference on Population, and it favours expanded support to increase contraceptive use. Increasingly, policy statements indicate the government considers its population problem to be extremely serious, particularly in relation to alleviating poverty. The basic aim of the government's population policy is to reduce fertility by influencing social variables known to promote fertility reduction, such as health, education and literacy, as well as by implementing a nationwide family planning programme. The government also perceives the population's spatial distribution to be inappropriate and it has adopted policies to reduce imbalances in population distribution in relation to natural resources, as well as congestion in urban areas.

Under the fifth five-year national development plan (1980-84), family planning continued to be accorded high priority, with emphasis on programme integration and coordination of activities involving all ministries and departments. During the sixth plan, the government sought to extend the delivery of services through the strengthening of health and family planning infrastructure, particularly rural infrastructure, with the aim of making family planning services available on a wider scale and at all levels.

Though statistics from contraceptive prevalence surveys are dated, they reveal that whereas 95 per cent of married women knew of some contraceptive method in the early 1980s, only 34 per cent were using any method at all.[233] Again, in a country as populous and poor as India, the success of its population policies and family planning programmes will be highly contingent on financial and human resources needed to extend its present services. Priorities include upgrading the service delivery capacity of the health care and family welfare network through intensive area development projects; strengthening the data collection and analysis system on interrelationships between population, environment and sustainable development; and strengthening the managerial capability at all levels of India's population programme through training, research, and the development and improvement of management information and evaluation systems.

A great deal needs to be done to support India's population education programme, both in and out of schools; and to produce additional audio-visual and printed materials for motivation campaigns. Most importantly, additional support for health and family welfare programmes aimed specifically at women should be developed, through innovative projects which emphasize the positive role women play as managers of reproduction as well as of natural resources required in everyday household use, notably fuelwood, water, and food security.

THE PHILIPPINES

Possessing much mountainous terrain, made up of fragile soils, and subjected to heavy tropical rainfall, the Philippines is unusually susceptible to environmental degradation, particularly soil erosion and associated disruption of watersheds. The situation is exacerbated by poverty, inequitable land distribution, a faltering economy, poor development policies, burdensome debt and rapid population growth. Indeed, the country has already undergone much environmental decline, notably in the form of deforestation, soil erosion, watershed abuse, disruption of water systems, over-harvesting of fisheries and destruction of mangroves and coral reefs.[28,46,261,262]

This is all the more regrettable in that the Philippines' economy is sustained in major measure by its natural resource base – soil cover, vegetation (especially forests), and water stocks. The sectors of agriculture, forestry and fisheries together contribute at least a quarter of GNP, earn two fifths of export revenues and employ half the labour force.[263] More than 60 per cent of Filipinos live in rural areas.

There are two factors central to the Philippine environment and economy. The first factor is the shortage of agricultural land. Nationwide, the amount of arable land per rural inhabitant has now declined to only 0.38 of a hectare (which means that an average family of six persons must try to sustain itself on only 2.28 hectares). Even this small amount may well fall by a further 40 per cent by the year 2000 to only 0.23 of a hectare per head. This small figure depends upon a population planning effort more vigorous than in the past several years, also upon a sizable increase in urban and off-farm employment. Yet to cope with population growth and nutritional needs, the country must achieve a 4 per cent annual increase in agricultural output – a questionable prospect given recent trends.

The second factor, closely related to the first, is that 55 per cent of the country is hilly or mountainous, which makes it all the more vulnerable to soil erosion. Within these uplands, 46 per cent feature 18 to 30 degree slopes, making them unsuitable for agriculture without exceptional soil-safeguard measures. Remaining uplands available for agricultural settlement are fast being claimed by a rising tide of immigrants from the "overcrowded" lowlands. While the agricultural frontier as conventionally defined was closed a good while ago in the lowlands, a similar frontier is now being closed in the uplands too – bringing on the prospect of a marked increase in agricultural settlement of steeply sloping land and along overcrowded coasts.[46] In other words, there is a "threshold effect" impending. While population growth has ostensibly been sustainable to date, albeit with long-term costs, it will shortly induce exceptionally severe burdens on the country's natural resource base.

These two key factors of the Philippines' environment are exemplified by the loss of forests. Almost all remaining forests are located in the uplands, constituting 22 per cent of national territory, though with the most productive old-growth dipterocarp forests now amounting to only 3 per cent.[264,265] At recent rates of cutting, the stocks will shortly be unable to satisfy domestic demands, let alone export markets. The 1984 output of logs and lumber slumped to the 1955 level; and whereas the export of logs and lumber in 1967 amounted to 32 per cent of all exports, in 1986 it was worth only 5 per cent.[266] Worse, there is a timber famine in the making. Domestic demand for timber, even if held to the current inadequate level of per capita consumption, is projected to exceed the 1985 amount by 69 per cent in the year 2000 and by 783 per cent in the year 2035.[265]

In the last two decades, the uplands have had to accommodate growing throngs of migrants from the lowlands.[267] The uplands population now totals more than 20 million people, or almost a third of all Filipinos. This flood of migrants has led to much deforestation among other forms of environmental degradation; and a good number of farms are on slopes as steep as 45 degrees. Many of the immigrants are below the official poverty line, so they cannot afford to deploy conservation technologies or make investments with long-term payoffs. Lacking security of tenure in their farmlands, they have scant access to credit.

Population projections indicate that, by the end of the century, all available arable land in the uplands will be occupied by small-scale cultivators, and a large additional amount of steeply-sloping land will be under cultivation too. This means that virtually all significant forest cover remaining today, whether of good or moderate quality, will have been removed. In turn, this means that the country's major hydrological systems, notably those of the so-called critical watersheds, will have been severely disrupted, with ecological repercussions such as flooding and sedimentation reaching across much of the lowlands and into near-shore areas. All in all, the mass movement of people into the uplands, extending over just a few decades, may eventually come to rank as one of the pivotal events in Philippine history.

Preliminary estimates suggest that more than 90,000 square kilometres of the country's uplands are so badly eroded that they can barely support subsistence agriculture; in many areas no crops can be grown at all.[268,269] In addition, there are the off-site costs of soil erosion, mainly related to the decline of watershed functions. At least 16,000 square kilometres of deforested uplands are located in watersheds that are critical for dependable water supplies of sufficient quantity and quality to feed hydropower facilities, irrigation projects and domestic needs in urban areas.[270] This is all the more significant in light of the country's plans for irrigated agriculture.[267] During the last quarter of this century, irrigation demand for water is projected to double if the country is to expand its irrigation systems from 14,000 square kilometres to 20,000 square kilometres (eventually projected to reach 31,000 square kilometres) out of total cultivable land of 90,000 square kilometres. So there is a premium on further efforts to safeguard water catchments through reforestation. Yet less than 200 square kilometres of uplands are reforested annually, out of the 1,000 square kilometres needed.

Meanwhile, the Philippines suffers from ever growing water deficits for agriculture. Since 1968, the areas affected have expanded from 812 square kilometres to almost 14,000 square kilometres. In 1983, the country suffered a modest failure of the monsoon, whereupon it experienced the most extensive and protracted drought in 30 years – 14,000 square kilometres of agricultural lands were affected, with production losses estimated at 1.3 million tonnes of grain.

With a coastline longer than that of the United States, the Philippines possesses extensive coastal and off-shore waters. With more than 22,000 kilometres of coral reefs and extensive seagrass beds and mangroves, the country's fisheries have been unusually fecund, supporting a quarter of the population.[46,271,272] Unfortunately, this is no longer the case. Decades of unfettered coastal development, involving the widespread destruction of lowland forests and mangrove swamps, and the rapid expansion of fish ponds, and together with the degradation of upland watersheds, have grossly depleted the fisheries. Coupled to this broad-scope impoverishment of coastal-zone ecosystems is a population growth rate that hovers between 2.5 and 3 per cent a year. Population pressures along coastlines are already over-taxing the natural resource base needed to support present human communities.[46]

The fish catch has now levelled off to around 2 million tonnes a year, probably amounting to maximum sustainable yield. Still, fish consumption per head is greater than any other Southeast Asian nation. Yet projections of future consumption indicate that by the year 2000, 83 million Filipinos are likely to be demanding more than 3 million tonnes of fish, and by 2020, 118 million people will require more than 4 million tonnes. Meanwhile, fish stocks continue to be depleted at rapid rates. Stocks of demersal fishes have been reduced to less than 30 per cent of their 1947 biomass levels, and the economic loss via "rent dissipation" of over-exploitation of these fisheries could be as much as $90 million annually.[272] Worse still, the Philippines' coastal crisis means that millions of small-scale commercial and subsistence fishermen can no longer make a minimum living from the sea without exploiting remaining stocks and employing illegal fishing techniques such as dynamite, poisons and fine-mesh nets.

All of these problems are aggravated to a severe degree by population growth. To avoid the implications of constant fertility between 1990 and 2025, meaning a burgeoning population in excess of 160 million by 2025, the crude birth rate of 35 per 1,000 in 1990 must decline substantially. To achieve the United Nations "medium variant" projection of 112 million people by 2025 will require a decline in the crude birth rate from 33-35 per 1,000 in 1990 to about 17 per 1,000 by 2025. To achieve the United Nations "low variant" projection of 102 million will require a birth rate of 13 per 1,000 by 2025.

As in the case of Pakistan and India, the Philippines government also perceives its population growth as "too high", and favours lowering fertility rates through support to family planning services. In addition, the government has become increasingly aware that the spatial distribution patterns of its population are too weighted toward urban areas and coastal zones. Halting the mass exodus from rural to urban areas and coastlines is now a high priority.

In 1987, the government approved a new National Population Policy. The population strategy has two major thrusts: a family planning and responsible parenthood programme, and an integrated population and development programme. The first seeks to extend the coverage of the family planning programme over the period 1989 to 1993 to include an additional 1.5 million eligible couples who want to practise family planning, while continuing to serve the 3.8 million couples already covered. The second aims to promote the integration of population concerns into development programmes and projects; and to ensure that the well-being of the individual and the family are fully addressed throughout development planning.

As an indication of the challenges involved, contraceptive prevalence surveys in 1983 revealed that 77 per cent of married women knew of some contraceptive method. Yet the percentage of women using contraceptives increased from only 38 per cent in 1978 to 45 per cent in 1986. Clearly, the government has a long way to go to realize its policy of stringently reduced population growth rates. To do so, it plans to expand family planning motivation as well as service delivery to cover the huge unmet need for family planning services and to integrate population concerns into all regional development plans. It is imperative that population growth and distribution be balanced with available resources and special attention paid to vulnerable ecological zones (such as upland forests, estuaries, mangroves, and coral reefs). In turn, greater efforts will be required to integrate population and environment issues into nationwide conservation strategies. Ultimately, the success of such efforts depends on increased financial and political support, strengthening of existing institutions, and the incorporation of the population dimension into national, regional and local development planning.

ETHIOPIA

Ethiopia, and the next country to be considered, Kenya, are symptomatic of many problems suffered by sub-Saharan Africa as a whole, even though Ethiopia is one of the most impoverished of nations while Kenya is frequently regarded as something of a development success story in the region. Both display many of the adverse repercussions of rapid population growth. But before examining these two countries in detail, and in order to supply a conceptual context for the entire region, let us take stock of some pervasive factors afflicting sub-Saharan Africa as a whole.

Of the region's nearly 450 million people in 1985, some 250 million were chronically malnourished; 150 million were subject to acute food deficits; and 30 million were actually starving.[273] In much if not most of the region, per capita food production has been declining for a full two decades. At least 62 per cent of the entire populace endures absolute poverty. As much as 80 per cent of croplands and 90 per cent of stock-raising lands are affected to some degree by land degradation processes.[159] Yet the population of sub-Saharan Africa, with an annual average growth rate of 3 per cent in 1985-90, is projected to reach 722 million by the year 2000 and almost 1.4 billion by 2025, according to the United Nations "medium variant" projection. This ultra-rapid rate of growth operates in conjunction with adverse climatic conditions, characterized by erratic rainfall patterns, frequent droughts and increasing desertification, that have affected the region for most of the past two decades.

Sub-Saharan Africa has continued to feature a fertility rate higher than anywhere else in the world; and since 1960, the region has been growing poorer and hungrier in absolute as well as relative terms. Today's average per capita income of roughly $250 is only 95 per cent of real income in 1960; of the 36 poorest countries in the world, 29 are in Africa.[274,275] Worse, average per capita agricultural production has declined by an average of 2 per cent annually since 1970 And the World Bank estimates that production is unlikely to grow at more than 2.5 per cent a year for at least the next two decades, even while population growth remains at 3 per cent or more a year.[276] As a result, food output per head, which has declined by 20 per cent since 1970, is scheduled to decline by a further 30 per cent during the next 25 years.[277-279] The region serves as a prime example of an "adverse outlook" scenario.[102,159,273,280-284]

In recent years there has been some respite, thanks to better rains. But because of unpromising baseline conditions generally, and particularly in respect to harsh climate,[82] together with widespread environmental degradation and poor agricultural policies, the return of only moderately adverse weather conditions could quickly trigger a renewed onset of broad-scale famine. If these adverse conditions persist – aggravated, perhaps, by the climatic vicissitudes entrained by the greenhouse effect – the number of chronically malnourished, which totalled 30 million in 1985, could well increase to 130 million by the end of this century.[285-287] This means that the proportion of starving people would expand from less than 7 per cent of the region's population in 1985 to 18 per cent by the year 2000.

It is within the context of sub-Saharan Africa as a whole that we should examine the case of Ethiopia. It epitomizes those nations with high population growth rates that must work exceptionally hard to satisfy their basic needs – food, water, shelter, health care, employment and education. When a nation is economically impoverished, it may well find the task all but beyond its means. So human needs overtake the pace of development, until eventually they

SUB-SAHARAN AFRICA: GROWTH RATES OF PER CAPITA
FOOD PRODUCTION AND LEVELS OF FOOD IMPORTS

Selected countries	Growth of per capita food production (per cent)			Level of food imports (millions of $)			
	1961-70	1971-79	1980-84	1961	1970	1980	1985
Western Africa							
Côte d'Ivoire	4.8	0.4	-1.5	38	82	487	422
Ghana	0.8	-3.5	-0.8	61	77	132	215
Mali	-0.3	-0.8	-1.6	8	17	70	82
Niger	-1.7	0.0	-5.7	3	9	82	45
Nigeria	0.2	-0.7	-1.6	90	127	2,085	1,524
Eastern Africa							
Burundi	-0.3	0.0	-3.0	1	4	30	24
Ethiopia	2.4	-1.6	-3.9	8	17	106	158
Kenya	0.1	-1.6	-2.0	41	50	214	153
Mozambique	0.9	-3.6	-3.9	21	37	114	84
Rwanda	2.6	0.4	-1.2	1	4	44	40
Somalia	0.5	-4.6	-4.1	12	16	147	164
Sudan	2.2	0.4	-3.6	41	65	390	203
Tanzania	2.6	-0.7	-3.4	31	32	16	101
Uganda	0.7	-1.2	0.7	15	21	45	18
Zambia	-0.2	-1.9	-2.4	20	48	145	68
Zimbabwe	2.3	-2.8	-7.9	12	11	62	40
Middle Africa							
Angola	1.0	-2.2	-2.2	25	56	268	211
Cameroon	1.4	-0.5	-2.1	14	31	131	152
Zaire	1.3	-1.5	0.6	27	63	166	147

threaten the very structure and stability of the nation. In Ethiopia, the
essentials of everyday life, in terms of food supplies alone, are
increasingly maintained by outside agencies rather than by the
government. The country's output of cereal grain in 1980, 5.1 million
tonnes, has been theoretically projected to expand to 7.3 million
tonnes in 1991 – though in fact, food production declined by an
average of 1 per cent a year during the 1980s.[102] Despite this projected
increase in cereal-grain output in 1991 to 7.3 million tonnes, Ethiopia's
need for cereal imports jumped from 214,000 tonnes in 1980 to more
than 3 million tonnes by 1991.

As a consequence of the severe imbalance between population and food supplies, plus associated political upheavals, there are now at least 5 million people facing starvation, and a total of almost 15 million people – nearly a third of the population – chronically undernourished. Furthermore, there are now at least 3 million displaced people within Ethiopia, and another half million in refugee camps in the Sudan (where they are explicitly recognized as environmental refugees rather than political refugees).

How did Ethiopia get to this state? By the early 1970s, as much as 470,000 square kilometres of Ethiopia's traditional farming areas in the highlands – home to 88 per cent of the population – were severely eroded. These formerly fertile upland areas were losing an estimated billion tonnes of topsoil a year (a more recent and refined estimate puts the loss at 1.5 to 3.5 billion tonnes a year).[288] This massive soil erosion was due partly to rudimentary agricultural practices, partly to inequitable land-tenure systems, and partly to pressures generated by a population that increased from 20 million in 1950 to 31 million by 1970. The results included a marked fall-off in agricultural production accompanied by food shortages in cities, with ensuing disorders that precipitated the overthrow of Emperor Hailie Selassie in 1974.[289-291]

The Dergue regime did not move fast enough to restore agricultural production.[292-296] Primarily for this reason, throngs of impoverished peasants started to stream into the country's lowlands, including the Ogaden zone that borders Somalia – a zone of long-standing conflict between the two nations. In Somalia, too, steadily increasing human numbers, together with inefficient agricultural practices, had led to much over-taxing of traditional farmlands. Largely for these reasons (plus some ethnic complications), there was a migration into the Ogaden from the Somali side as well. The result was a clash between the two sides, with an outbreak of hostilities in 1977.[297,298]

Primarily as a result of a regional arms race and internal conflicts, Ethiopia in 1981 spent $447 million on defence, and Somalia $105 million. Added to the outlays of previous years, the total sum expended in the Horn of Africa because of the Ogaden conflict can be estimated at well over $1 billion during a five-year period.[299] If only a small part of that sum had been allocated ahead of time to reforestation, soil safeguards and associated aspects of restoring the agricultural resource base in the two countries – estimated by the United Nations Anti-Desertification Plan to cost no more than $50 million a year for 10 years – the disastrous outcome could well have been avoided.

Environmental breakdown and food shortages have now become

endemic in Ethiopia.[300] The mid-1980s drought was no more than a triggering factor, precipitating a crisis that had been building up for decades through the pressure of population growth and agricultural mismanagement.[301,302] To relieve these longer-term crises, there is need for agricultural development inputs to be doubled, soil conservation and other environmental programmes to be increased four-fold, livestock husbandry to be expanded six-fold, and population planning activities to be increased sufficiently in order to limit the ultimate population.[288,303]

According to the United Nations "constant fertility variant" projection, if crude birth rates were to remain at 1990 levels over the next 45 years, total population would increase from 49 million in 1990 to 161 million by 2025. Were crude birth rates brought more into line with the UN "medium variation" projection – requiring a birth-rate decline from 49 per 1,000 in 1985-90 to about 30 per 1,000 in 2020-25 – the total population would grow far less, to about 127 million by 2025.

Between 1974 and 1980, the government of Ethiopia perceived its rates of population growth and fertility as "satisfactory", requiring no intervention. Furthermore, it provided little support for family planning services. More recently, the government has changed its position, now viewing population growth and fertility levels as being "not satisfactory" because they are "too high" in relation to family well-being and in particular to maternal and child health. While family planning services were initiated by the Ministry of Health in 1981, only 23 per cent of the country's 2,500 health stations, centres and hospitals provided integrated maternal, child health and family planning services. In 1981, the contraceptive prevalence rate was estimated to be only 2 per cent, more recent estimates suggest rates of 2 to 8 per cent in urban areas and from 1 to 2 per cent in rural areas.

Government priorities include the formulation of a more focused population policy which rationalizes current population growth patterns relative to the country's economic and environmental carrying capacity. Furthermore, in view of the extensive poverty in the country, and limited resources available to the government for population activities, various forms of assistance are urgently needed to strengthen Ethiopia's existing population programme. These include strengthening the national maternal and child health care programme as part of the government's family welfare goals; greatly expanded population education on relationships between population, environment and sustainable development in primary and secondary schools, as well as in non-formal education; strengthening national capacities for population analysis, studies and training in Ethiopia's major universities and research-oriented non-governmental organizations; and programmes to support and encourage the potential of women in their role as natural resource managers.

The Dergue government, like the Selassie regime before it, has been unable to resolve the problem of growing human numbers seeking to survive off an impoverished natural resource base. Even though Ethiopia has had one of the lowest population growth rates in sub-Saharan Africa – around 2 per cent a year for most of the time between 1950 and 1980, rising to 2.9 per cent in 1990 – Ethiopia's population had increased from 20 million in 1950 to about 49 million by 1990.[304]

KENYA

Kenya's economic performance since independence in 1963 has surpassed that of virtually all other sub-Saharan countries. But the benefits of a strongly growing GNP have been markedly reduced by population growth. During the late 1980s, the growth rate was 3.6 per cent a year, one of the highest levels ever recorded for natural increase in a single country. By 1990, it had risen to 3.7 per cent, meaning that the current total of 24.9 million would double in little over 18 years. Because of the "youthful profile" of its population pyramid (54 per cent of people are under the age of 16, by contrast with 22 per cent in developed countries), there is much demographic momentum built into Kenya's population future. Even were the family size to come down to two children forthwith, the population would still keep on growing for another two generations at least, and double in size before attaining zero growth. As it is, the present population of 25 million is projected to surpass 35 million by 2000, before expanding to 79 million by 2025.[16]

Yet the Food and Agriculture Organization's study on population supporting capacities postulates that even with high-level farming inputs the country could not feed more than 51 million people from its land resources.[29] Meantime, agricultural production averaged only a 3.5 per cent annual growth rate during the 1980s, well below the population growth rate of 3.6 per cent or higher. As a result, per capita agricultural output has been falling: with an index of 100 in 1976-78, it slumped to 87 in 1985,[305] and it has been declining even more since then.[306] More than 30 per cent of the population suffers from nutritional deficiencies.[307] Agricultural production must be doubled from 1982 levels by the end of the century, simply to keep up with population growth.[308] Between 1975 and 1984 annual food aid in cereals jumped from 4,000 tonnes to 209,000 tonnes.

A main reason why agricultural production has been declining is that the environmental support base has been overloaded by fast-rising human numbers in the rural areas where 85 per cent of the population lives.[306] Despite a strong soil-conservation effort, most farmland areas have long featured soil erosion to some degree; in several densely populated areas, potential food output could eventually decline by as much as 50 per cent if soil loss cannot be reversed.[309] Severe desertification has already overtaken 19 per cent of the country and is spreading fast.[310] Forests have been reduced to 3 per cent of national territory, precipitating gross disruption of watershed flows to valleyland farming areas.

This environmental rundown affects sectors other than agriculture. Deforestation is triggering a crisis in energy. Fuelwood and charcoal account for 73 per cent of energy supplies nationwide, and at least 95 per cent of all wood cut is for this purpose. But as forests diminish, the prospect is that demand for fuelwood and charcoal in the year 2000 will be three times greater than can be supplied through incremental wood growth.[311-313]

As rural populations find it difficult to subsist off increasingly subdivided farms, there is an influx of migrants into urban areas causing cities to swell by 8 per cent a year, almost twice the national population growth rate. To avoid any increase in unemployment and underemployment, now estimated at more than 40 per cent of the workforce, the country will have to double the number of jobs between 1985 and the end of this century.[314,315] To achieve this will require an economic growth rate of 8 per cent a year rather than the recent 5.5 per cent rate.

Overall there must be a doubling of all manner of facilities and services – schools, teachers, health centres, doctors, administrators and the like – every 18 years merely to keep abreast of an annual population growth rate of 3.7 per cent. That the nation has hardly managed to keep up with the challenge (even with a smaller population growth rate) is demonstrated by the fact that its per capita GNP has shown hardly any advance for the great majority of people since 1970, and most have less to eat today than at the time of independence in 1963. The mutually reinforcing problems of population growth and environmental decline are further compounded by the lack of socio-economic infrastructure: too few trained leaders, professional staffers and general managers, and too few of all these in almost every sector and at almost every level.[316] Despite some recent admirable efforts to foster family planning, leading to a sudden decline in the total fertility rate from over 8 to under 7, demographic inertia from exceptionally high population growth rates in the past means that Kenya will face still greater difficulties if it is merely to hold the line on living standards.[317]

What then are the prospects for reducing future rates of population growth in Kenya? The United Nations "medium variant" projection – implying a drop in the birth rate from about 47 per 1,000 in 1985-90 to about 29 per 1,000 in 2020-25 will still produce a daunting outcome of 79 million people by 2025.

Fortunately, the government of Kenya recognizes the difficulties involved. It has long considered levels and trends of population growth and fertility to be unsatisfactory because they are "too high": high fertility is viewed as impeding development efforts. The government also views current population distribution patterns as only partially appropriate, especially because rapid urban expansion is believed to contribute to the growth of slums and excessive demand for urban services. The government is also concerned about the imbalances between urban and rural development, and about the regional disparities in living standards.

Accordingly, Kenya became the first sub-Saharan country to adopt an official population policy, although this was not reflected in the national development plan until 1975. The major objective in this and in subsequent national development plans, has been to reduce the annual population growth rate through the delivery of family planning services from a network of service delivery points. However, there has been a manifest shortfall in achieving this fertility reduction objective, even as the government has sought to expand services throughout the country. Kenya's contraceptive prevalence survey has shown that 80 per cent of women knew of at least one method of family planning in 1984, but only 15 per cent of reproductive age women were actually using any contraceptive methods at all.[233]

The government has also sought to implement spatial redistribution policies and has established a sectoral planning group on population (1984-88) to ensure incorporation of demographic data into the development planning process. Population policy and related matters are centralized in the National Council for Population and Development which is based in the Office of the Vice-President and the Ministry of Home Affairs.

To say that an easy recipe of population policies and programmes can be devised to accelerate population decline in Kenya would be to ignore the many complexities of the situation. This applies particularly to factors influencing demand, as well as traditional financial constraints on supply. However, various assessments of basic needs and shortfalls in the country suggest the following. First, the demand for family planning needs to be stimulated through a multi-sectoral and decentralized district-level approach to population information, education and communication activities. This will be especially important as regards awareness creation about important linkages between rapid population growth, unbalanced population distribution and environmental degradation. Second, greater understanding is required of social, economic and cultural factors which are sustaining high family size; this requires synthesis of on-going anthropological and sociological research on the subject, as well as translation of such knowledge into action-oriented programmes. Third, efforts to improve women's status, particularly education, employment opportunities, and legal provisions, are crucial, especially as such improvements have both direct and indirect effects on family welfare and family size.

MEXICO

Mexico is more of a middle-income country than the others considered thus far, with a current per capita income of $1,800. But it still illustrates the problems of population growth with respect to environment, albeit problems of a rather different sort from those already reviewed.[318-322]

Mexico was the first developing country to engage in Green Revolution agriculture, expanding its grain production four-fold between the mid-1950s and the mid-1980s. But its population growth has also been among the most rapid anywhere, increasing from 28 million in 1950 to 89 million by 1990 (a 218 per cent increase), making it the second largest populace in Latin America. As a result of the upsurge in human numbers and nutritional needs, plus an increase in environmental degradation, the benefits of the Green Revolution breakthroughs have all but dwindled away in terms of per capita consumption. Mexico has once again become a net food importer.

Because much of the country is dry, it possesses limited agricultural land.[323-325] In more than 70 per cent of these lands, soil erosion is significant: 60 per cent medium and growing worse, 12 per cent severe.[326,327] Outright desertification claims 2,250 square kilometres of farmlands each year.[74] At least one tenth of irrigated areas have become highly salinized, and 10,000 square kilometres need urgent (and expensive) rehabilitation if they are to be restored to productivity.

Moreover, the country's remaining forests total only 120,000 square kilometres, and are giving way to large-scale ranchers and small-scale peasants alike. The loss of the forests' "sponge effect" disrupts river flows: in two thirds of arable lands, water supplies constitute the main factor that is limiting agricultural productivity.[328] Because of dwindling water supplies, together with soil erosion, at least 1,000 square kilometres of farmlands are abandoned each year.[329] From the late 1950s to the early 1970s, the area under staple crops – corn, wheat, rice and beans – expanded by almost half, extending into marginal lands with highly erodible soils.[324,330] At least 45 per cent of all farmers occupy those 20 per cent of croplands located on steep slopes.[331] By the mid-1970s, these newly opened-up areas were starting to feature declining crop yields – precisely at the time when there was a peak in population growth. Domestic calorie production as a percentage of total supply reached 105 per cent in 1970 but, by 1982, it had slipped to 94 per cent.[332]

The distribution of agricultural lands is becoming ever more skewed as large farmers buy out small farmers and engage in capital-intensive cash cropping for export. But growing numbers of smallholder peasants impose still greater strains on over-worked croplands, reducing their carrying capacity; and migrating throngs of marginalized farmers are pushed into those lands most susceptible to degradation.[333,334]

As a result of this agricultural squeeze, there has been a recent upsurge in migration from Mexico's rural areas.[335-338] Many migrants head for Mexico's cities which, after growing at 5 per cent or more a year since 1960, are less and less capable of absorbing new arrivals. For every two rural Mexicans who migrate to the city, one now crosses the border into the United States.[339,340]

What are some likely future population pressures in Mexico? Despite a remarkable economic performance for much of the period 1960 to 1980, average real wages in 1988 were below the level of 1970; and the economy has generally stagnated or even contracted since 1980 while the population has grown by more than a quarter. Nor does the economic outlook presage much improvement.[341] A realistic prognosis is that within a decade Mexicans could well be poorer than they are today.[342,343] Just to keep pace with a swelling work force, Mexico will have to create jobs at half the rate the United States achieves, while doing it within an economy only one thirtieth the size, and at an investment cost that could conceivably reach $500 billion by the year 2000.[344] This is an unrealistic expectation. In 1986, a year with poor economic performance because of declining oil prices and growing debt burden, the jobs total actually decreased. Not surprisingly, then, it is an optimistic estimate that foresees "only" 20 million Mexicans without proper employment by the turn of the century. At least half of these will be living in rural areas, where there could be an additional 2 million, perhaps even 4 million, landless peasants. According to Professor J. G. Castañeda of the National University of Mexico, "The consequences of not creating nearly 15 million jobs in the next 15 years are unthinkable. The youths who do not find them will have only three options: the United States, the streets or revolution."[342]

The biggest issues confronting Mexico appear to be population growth and urbanization. The population could more than double between 1990 and 2025 if fertility rates were to remain unchanged. Realizing the United Nations "medium variant" projection – implying a drop in the crude birth rate from 28 per 1,000 in 1990 to about 18 per 1,000 in 2025 – would still result in a population of 150 million by 2025, up from 89 million in 1990. Bolder reductions, to achieve the UN "low variant" projection, would imply a further drop in the birth rate to 15 per 1,000 in 2025, resulting in a total population of 132 million.

Since 1974, the government of Mexico has considered its rates of population growth to be "too high", and has promoted policies to lower growth rates, chiefly through fertility reduction by providing support to contraceptive information, education, and supplies. The government has consistently expressed dissatisfaction with imbalances in the growth and distribution of population (including migration patterns), in relation to the distribution of natural resources. In view of these policies, the government has taken steps to integrate specific demographic goals into its overall development planning. In 1974, Mexico adopted a General Population Law with the aim of regulating factors affecting population structure, volume, dynamics and distribution, and it established the National Population Council (CONAPO), which is responsible for formulating plans on population and promoting their integration into economic and social programmes. In 1977, the country approved a national family planning policy with the aim of reducing the population growth rate; and in 1979, a regional population policy was adopted, addressed to the specific problems of interregional migration and the geographical distribution of the population.[345]

By 1987, approximately 91 per cent of married women knew of at least one contraceptive method, while 53 per cent were actually using one method or another. On the one hand, this indicates considerable progress since the contraceptive prevalence rate was only about 30 per cent in 1976, grew to 48 per cent by 1982 and has now passed 50 per cent. On the other hand, approximately 45 per cent of married women have yet to be reached by family planning programmes – an important goal in view of population and environmental problems.

Recognizing the urgency of the problems at hand, the government is now embarking on several aggressive strategies and programmes to enhance the effectiveness of its population policies. For example, it seeks to reduce the population growth rate to 1.8 per cent by 1994 and to 1 per cent by the year 2000. In order to achieve a better distribution of population, more in line with the development potential of different regions, the government aims to lessen the relative size of the great metropolitan zones and to encourage the growth of small and intermediate cities. The government also seeks to promote the integration of demographic objectives and criteria more explicitly into the country's economic and social planning; and it aims to raise the socio-economic status and role of women as contributors to the economy and as environmental managers.

EL SALVADOR

El Salvador contains about 5.3 million people on 21,400 square kilometres of land, a population density higher than that of any other nation in Central America. It also suffers more environmental degradation than any other nation, notably through soil erosion, deforestation and depletion of water supplies. The first certainly contributes to the second, while acting in concert with other factors such as inequitable land-tenure systems, disparities of wealth and income, and a repressive oligarchy.

About half of El Salvador's populace are farmers. So important is the environmental resource base to the economy that more than two thirds of export revenues have been derived from agricultural commodities.[97] Yet soil erosion is extensive and often severe. Forests are a matter of history. Watershed deterioration is the rule rather than the exception. Water flows from upland catchments are increasingly erratic, with adverse repercussions for irrigated agriculture in the lowlands. As a result of deteriorating agricultural resources, among other factors, the country is increasingly unable to feed itself. Per capita grain production declined from 142 kilograms in 1950 to 129 kilograms in 1983.[346]

Agriculture is also beset with maldistribution of farmlands, associated problems of land-tenure systems and, most of all, pressures of high population growth (2.2 per cent in 1990).[337] Cropland per person has fallen by more than two thirds since 1950, and agricultural advances – agrarian technology, credit systems, extension services – have not nearly compensated for such a steep falloff. Almost half of the country's farmers are confined to only 5 per cent of its agricultural lands, and the average smallholding is half a hectare or less. Almost two thirds of the farming community can be categorized as near-landless or landless.[212,347] As a result, throngs of impoverished peasants are pushed into marginal environments, often steep-sloped areas where the friable volcanic soil readily erodes.

Environmental degradation should be viewed within the context of a national economy that has been steadily declining for the past two decades. Per capita GDP in constant 1982 dollars amounted to $610 in 1960, rising to $785 in 1970 and to $855 in 1980, but falling to $708 in 1984 and to $690 in 1987.[348] Salvadorians today are economically worse off than they were in 1970 and little better off than in 1960. The economic decline is forcing large numbers of people to return to a state of semi-subsistence in which their main option is to exploit the meagre natural resources available.

The average population density of the country is well over 250 per square kilometre, exceeding that of India, and between three and 10 times greater than that of other countries in the region. Worse, it is projected to reach over 300 per square kilometre within eight or nine years. Thus, El Salvador experiences by far the most acute land pressures in Central America, even disallowing the skewed distribution of farmlands.

Clearly population growth and environmental decline are substantial contributors to the present debacle, together with maldistribution of land and the concentration of economic and political power in the landed oligarchy. As a result, there has been a steady migration of people into neighbouring countries. By the late 1960s, when El Salvador had an average of 158 persons per square kilometre and, by comparison, Honduras had only 57, one out of eight Salvadorians had migrated to Honduras. Tensions over this mass movement of people erupted in 1969 in the so-called Soccer War.[349] Since then more than 500,000 people have migrated to other Central American countries before migrating to countries further afield.[337] All told, some 20 per cent of Salvadorians, counting internally displaced as well as international refugees, have relinquished their homelands.[350] While political repression and inequitable social factors have often played a role, many of these migrants can legitimately be called environmental refugees.

Nor is the future any more promising. Such are the population pressures that even if the government's land reform programme begun in 1980 were fully successful, about a third of the rural poor would still not have secure access to farmland.[337,347] The 1990 population of 5.3 million is projected to reach 6.7 million by the year 2000 and 10.4 million by 2020. Yet the country could not support more than 10 million people through its own land resources even if it fully employs high-technology methods of agriculture.[29,351] Prospects for purchasing food abroad are also poor. Even projecting a highly optimistic economic growth rate of 3.9 per cent a year, the World Bank does not expect Salvadorians to enjoy the standard of living they had in 1979 – before the outbreak of the civil war – until the year 2006. With a more realistic growth rate for the economy of between 3 and 3.5 per cent a year, per capita income would continue to decline, failing to regain even its poor 1979 level. To make matters worse, half or more of new entrants into the job market would remain unemployed in the year 2006, thus adding further pressures to the natural resource base if they opted for a semi-subsistence lifestyle in marginal lands.

Population growth and distribution therefore take on paramount importance, given the country's economic and environmental carrying capacity. The United Nations "medium variant" projection implies a reduction in crude birth rates from about 36 per 1,000 in 1985-90 to 24 per 1,000 in 2020-25, in which case the total population would grow to about 11 million by 2025. Were fertility levels to be commensurate with the UN "low variant" – meaning a crude birth rate of about 21 per 1,000 – the total population would reach 10 million by 2025.[352]

As with most of the countries reviewed thus far, the government has consistently perceived population growth rates as "too high" since the 1974 World Population Conference. As of 1976, the country has sought lower fertility by providing direct support to contraceptive information, education and supplies. It views its spatial distribution as inappropriate, and has sought to implement policies to help correct population imbalances in relation to available natural resources. The government of El Salvador has adopted measures to help reduce population growth rates by improving maternal and child health care, increasing employment opportunities, strengthening nutrition and immunization programmes, and improving educational standards and the status of women. As regards unmanageable urban growth, the government has also adopted strategies to slow the growth of its principal city, San Salvador, and it has pursued rural development schemes designed to make rural areas more attractive places to live and work. To date, however, the government has not established quantitative targets for the reduction of population growth.

Progress has been made on the population front, but challenges remain. Perhaps nothing better illustrates this than the results of the United Nations survey on contraceptive prevalence rates in the mid-to-late 1980s. The percentage of married women who knew of one or more contraceptive methods was about 93 per cent in 1985, but only 47 per cent of them were using any contraceptives.[233] This contrasts favourably however with a contraceptive prevalence rate of only 22 per cent in 1975. Nevertheless, the results indicate that upwards of 50 per cent of married women have yet to be reached by family planning services.[199]

In relation to population, El Salvador's priorities are to continue to expand its service infrastructure, to bolster its national capacity in policy analysis, research and data collection, and to help foster fuller integration of population factors into national planning. This will require increased financial and human resources to support El Salvador's Ministry of Health in its efforts to improve the quality and coverage of maternal and child health and family planning. At the same time, the Population Department in the Ministry of Planning will have to be strengthened, along with agencies involved in data collection and analysis, such as the General Directorate of Statistics, universities and non-governmental agencies. The government's population efforts will further benefit by far more extensive programmes to improve population education in schools and in the non-formal educational sector, together with programmes to enhance women's educational, productive and environmental activities.

CHAPTER 4

POLICY RESPONSES

Problems of population growth and environmental decline demand urgent attention. In many instances they can still be turned around, into exceptional opportunities for counter-measures, both remedial and preventive. Of course, a spectrum of issues will be involved, including the innovation and dissemination of less polluting technologies; concentrated efforts by local, national and international agents to clean up wastes and improve waste disposal; conservation measures to protect marginal and common lands, to promote reforestation, and to protect fisheries; clarification of land tenure and adoption of agrarian reform; and far more pervasive measures to tackle poverty. Equally important are policies to promote a more balanced distribution of population to natural resources, between geographical regions and rural/urban sectors; and measures to plan for, service and reduce population growth and its demands on the natural resource base.

There is plenty of scope for timely and incisive interventions on the part of policy makers, with a highly positive payoff extending into the indefinite future. But time is at a premium. The decisive period for response will surely be confined for the most part to the 1990s. Thereafter, there will be much less manoeuvring room for policy interventions. We shall be left with a prospect where we can achieve much less at far greater cost.

This concluding chapter sets out some principal options for policy responses in the population and environment domain. Several are reflected in the Declaration of the International Forum on Population in the Twenty-first Century (Amsterdam, November 1989), agreed to by representatives of 79 countries. Solutions to global environmental problems will be possible only if all governments participate in identifying population and environment linkages and act, accordingly, to resolve them. Governments should therefore ensure that:
• Development planning takes into account environmental considerations in achieving population goals. Countries should identify areas with the most acute population pressures on the environment. Environmental problems of large cities in developing countries should receive special attention. Since economic development, population growth and distribution are interrelated, development plans should give special attention to population-related

The Amsterdam Declaration

The following goals and targets were adopted by the Amsterdam Forum on Population in the Twenty-first Century in November 1989.

The attainment of population goals and objectives should rest on seven main pillars:

- Strengthening political commitment.
- Development of national strategies and programmes.
- Acceleration and expansion of resource mobilization.
- Strengthening of the role and status of women.
- Strengthening of the quality, effectiveness and outreach of family planning and maternal and child health programmes and services in both the public and the private sectors.
- Heightening of community awareness and participation at all levels in the formulation and implementation of programmes and projects based on priorities and needs expressed by the women and men involved.
- Intensification of international cooperation in the sphere of population activities, specially directed and adapted to the specific conditions, particularly socio-cultural conditions, of recipient countries.

At the very least, national population goals and objectives for the coming decade and beyond should include:

- A reduction in the average number of children born per woman commensurate with achieving, as a minimum, the medium variant population projections of the United Nations.
- A major reduction in the proportion of women and men who are not currently using reliable methods of family planning, but who want to postpone, delay or limit childbearing.
- A substantial reduction in very early marriage and in teenage pregnancy.
- An increase in contraceptive prevalence in developing countries so as to reach at least 56 per cent of women of reproductive age by the year 2000.
- A reduction of the 1980 rate of infant mortality to rates of at most 50 per 1,000 live births by the year 2000 in all countries and major sub-groups within countries.
- A reduction in maternal mortality from all causes, including illegal abortion, by at least 50 per cent by the year 2000, particularly in regions where this figure currently exceeds 100 per 100,000 births.
- An increase in the average life expectancy at birth to 62 years or more for men and women in high mortality countries by the end of the century.
- A better geographical distribution of the population within national territories in balance with the proper use of resources.

UNFPA then called on the international donor community to increase funds for population activities from the current $3.5 billion a year to $9 billion a year by the turn of the century.

programmes aimed at improving environmental conditions at local levels, especially among the poorest sectors of the population.

• Significant changes in natural resources should be monitored and anticipated. This information should be fed back into development plans and related to the planning of spatial distribution of population.

• Land and water use as well as spatial planning should bring about a balanced distribution of population through, for example, incentives for industrial location and for resettlement and development of intermediate-sized towns, keeping in view the population carrying capacities of the environment.

• Public works, including food-for-work programmes, should be designed and implemented in areas of environmental stress and population pressures, with a view to providing employment and simultaneously improving the environment.

• Governments and voluntary organizations should increase public understanding, through formal and non-formal education, of the significance of population planning for environmental improvement and the important role of local action. The role of women in improving the environment and in population planning should receive special attention, as social changes that raise the status of women can have a profound effect on population variables, notably the reduction of fertility and a decline in population growth rates.

• Private enterprise, and industry in particular, should participate actively in the work of governments and non-governmental organizations aimed at ameliorating population and environmental stress.

• Education should be geared towards making people more capable of dealing with over-crowding and shrinking land holdings. Such education should help people acquire practical and vocational skills to enable them to become more self-reliant and enhance their participation in improving the environment at the local level.

In turn, these objectives will depend, as we shall now see, on population policy formulation; information and education media; responses to unmet needs in maternal and child health care and family planning; and enhancing women's status. Let us consider these in some detail.

ENHANCING CAPACITIES FOR POPULATION POLICY FORMULATION

First and foremost, all governments should develop the capacity to integrate population factors into development planning. At the outset, this requires a comprehensive assessment of trends in population growth and distribution, both present and projected. In particular, governments need to formulate answers to such key questions as the following. What size of population, and with what distribution patterns, will be engendered by a continuation of presently anticipated rates of growth? What effects will this have on the prospect for sustainable development? How far can sustainable development be fostered by reduced rates of growth and hence, how fast should rates of growth be brought down, and what scope is there (given population structures, age distributions and the like) for rapid and sustained reductions in growth rates? What time horizons are relevant in terms of reaching a "demographic transition", and when can zero growth (replacement level fertility) be achieved? And finally, what does each of these time horizons imply for population-planning measures (total fertility rate goals).

Central to these considerations is the question of demographic momentum. Incisive measures to curtail demographic momentum today will exert a compounding impact with progressively positive payoff for a long time into the future. Similarly, deferred action will lead to ever increasing inertia in growth rates, making future efforts to reduce numbers all the more difficult – more complex, more taxing, more costly, and with diminished payoff compared with investment. This question of demographic momentum is crucial to the formulation of population policies and planning, yet it often receives far less explicit and systematic attention than it deserves.

Moreover, population futures cannot be formulated in an "environmental vacuum". There are many intimate relationships between population growth – dependent as it inevitably is on carrying capacity – and the natural resource base that ultimately underpins all socio-economic endeavours and hence the scope for human communities to sustain themselves. This means that all population factors should be evaluated as part of national strategies with respect to their environmental linkages. What adverse impacts will be generated through continued population growth, manifest through overloading of agricultural lands, depletion of water supplies, decline of forests, spread of deserts, atmospheric pollution, depletion of the ozone layer and global warming? How far will all this undermine prospects for sustainable development? Conversely, how far will efforts to reduce population growth serve to safeguard the population carrying capacity of natural resource stocks?

The dictates of integrated policy formulation for population and environmental issues postulate a series of initiatives to translate policies into action.

Initiatives for enhanced policy analysis and planning include:

• A systematized evaluation of the multiple dynamic interactions between population and environment, in accord with the established spectrum of development sectors (agriculture, energy, industry, health, etc.) and in accord with the leading geographic areas (Asia, Africa, Latin America, humid zones, arid zones, coastal zones, montane ecosystems, urban areas, and so on). In addition, the impacts on the environment resource base imposed by "special interest" groups such as the bottom billion poorest and top billion richest should be analyzed in detail with particular emphasis on the key concept of population carrying capacity.

• An equally systematized evaluation of short-run and long-run targets as concerns population planning and environmental management, with explicit evaluation of payoffs both positive and negative.

Initiatives for improved planning include:

• Institutional measures to operationalize the policy decisions throughout government systems, for example, through the designation of lead agencies, working in conjunction with a link-up mechanism that ensures frequent and regular consultation between all agencies responsible for population and environment related activities. This can be accomplished by the establishment of a high-level coordinating body such as a National Population Commission, answerable directly to the office of the topmost governmental authority (usually the president or prime minister). At a more routine level, it can be facilitated by locating a Population Unit within the National Planning Ministry. More than 60 countries now have such units.

• Development of local expertise to monitor and evaluate the complex interrelationships between population, environment and sustainable development. Means to do so include training of national counterparts in projects involving international experts or consultants, technical seminars, study tours and fellowships for study abroad and, above all, development of local institutions – universities, government research institutes and non-governmental organizations specializing in the study of population and environment – to ensure a consistent supply of skills needed.

INFORMATION, EDUCATION, AND COMMUNICATION

To foster awareness of the critical links between population and environment, as well as initiatives to tackle them, there is a need to engage in nationwide information, education, and communication campaigns – from macro planning levels to the most micro of grassroots levels, from officialdom to business, commerce and the media, from national programmes to non-governmental organizations and local community leaders. All sectors of society should become thoroughly informed about the imperatives of population planning and environmental safeguards as key components of sustainable development.

Educational systems offer abundant scope to introduce communities of all ages to environmental concerns. An advantage of the formal schooling system is that many regular courses in the curriculum deal with issues bearing on the environment, many of them at sophisticated levels (for example, science courses). Increasingly, integrated curricula reveal key interrelationships between resources, environmental quality and population factors. If students are exposed to such information at an early age, there is a greater chance that they will grow up to be environmentally aware.

In addition, informal education on population and environment has advantages in that many courses offered are attuned to the "problems of the day", pose practical assessments, and are linked with grassroots or communal non-governmental organizations which have the potential for follow-up. Informal education also represents an important avenue for reaching people outside the formal schooling system – educated adults at work, dropouts and illiterates.

UNMET NEEDS IN MATERNAL AND CHILD HEALTH CARE AND FAMILY PLANNING

A prominent measure to promote sustainable development is to improve the quality of life of all citizens through human resource development. This further serves to foster environmental protection and conservation. While it is recognized by virtually all governments as a primary means to attain socio-economic development, it is not put into practice as widely and methodically as could be the case. One of the most productive options to enhance quality of life is to reduce morbidity and mortality, especially through maternal and child health care (MCH).

A readily available avenue to promote MCH lies in family planning. Services should be immediately accessible to all who need them. This will yield many benefits, such as reducing and ultimately eliminating all unwanted pregnancies; reducing the incidence of abortions, especially those conducted under unsupervised or inadequate professional medical help; and promoting birth spacing, which supports the health of both mothers and children alike.

An especially important factor in human resource development, with immense implications for environmental protection and hence for sustainable development, lies with the question of unmet needs in family planning. This refers to the needs of those women who possess the motivation for family planning, but lack access to contraceptives or other family planning services. Women whose choices are severely constrained because they lack access to family planning services, are estimated to total between 25 and 50 per cent of developing-country women of reproductive age. Insofar as it is a United Nations-recognized right for parents to have only the number of children they desire ("every child a wanted child"), they should be supplied with contraceptive services and better health facilities on humanitarian grounds alone. A policy initiative along these lines would reduce birth rates by as much as 27 per cent in Africa, 33 per cent in Asia and 35 per cent in Latin America. Indeed, it could cut the eventual global population by at least a billion people.[353] In turn, this would go far to relieve population pressures on natural resources and environmental systems.

Whereas international and national level initiatives can set the stage for action through research, analysis, planning, awareness creation and funding, it is at the local level that action-oriented projects will come directly into contact with unmet needs in family planning. Such needs can be accommodated by:

• Supplying family planning services and information at the local level, in addition to promoting longer time between pregnancies (child spacing gives both mother and child better chances of survival); delaying first births (obstructed labour claims the lives of many young girls between the ages of 12 and 17); and preventing child pregnancies.

• Providing both prenatal and postnatal care at the local level, emphasizing nutritional supplements for undernourished pregnant and lactating women, promoting breast-feeding and providing supplementary food, especially for malnourished teenage mothers in order to help reduce the incidence of low birth weight babies.

• Improving infant and child health to allow mothers to participate more fully in local level population and development activities.

• Educating women and men to be more aware of the need for sanitary treatment of food and drinking water, washing hands before meals, safe disposal of excreta, and other simple steps to improve family health and well-being.

These elements of successful and inexpensive health services have already had dramatic results. To apply them, however, health workers and basic supplies must be readily accessible, especially to poor households in rural communities and urban squatter settlements. So added requirements for strategic planning in this area are to:

• Create facilities in villages and urban neighbourhoods using paramedical personnel, with referral to, and supervision from, local medical centres.
• Expand outreach to every household, using workers recruited from the local community.
• Work with and through such local organizations as mothers' clubs.
• Integrate all services at the local level.
• Decentralize many aspects of programme management.

POPULATION DISTRIBUTION, MIGRATION AND URBANIZATION

Governments need to formulate policies to combat growing problems of population distribution, as manifested by the urban concentrations arising from massive migrations from rural areas to cities, especially mega-cities; Santiago, for example, accounts for a third of Chile's population on 2 per cent of its national territory.[354] This leads to acute imbalances in natural resource stocks to support the respective communities, with cities exerting a severely parasitic impact on their hinterlands.

In particular, governments should devise policies to defuse the many sources of migratory pressures which cause the urban-rural imbalance: a bias of development patterns favouring industry over agriculture and urban communities over rural communities; pricing mechanisms favouring urban consumers to the detriment of rural producers, reducing farmers' incentives to safeguard food-producing lands; lack of rural infrastructure; virtual absence of agrarian reform to correct maldistribution of farmlands; lack of land-tenure and ownership rights for small farmers; lack of extension services, credit systems and marketing networks to support small-scale agriculture; and mismanagement of common lands in rural areas.[355,356]

Fortunately these deficiencies are well known for the most part as are the measures required to correct the situation. The time has long been ripe for energetic interventions by policy makers – measures which would go far to relieve the population pressures and environmental degradation stemming from excessive rural-urban migration.

WOMEN'S STATUS

Closely related to all these instances of major policy interventions is the question of women's status in developing countries. There is much evidence to support the notion that development lags in those countries where fertility rates are slow to decline because women are denied the opportunity to enjoy a full productive life, especially as concerns health, education, work opportunities and their general social standing. There is also evidence that when women are accorded their proper place in society – a matter of basic equity anyway – they are quickly inclined to reduce their fertility levels. At the same time, emancipated, better-educated women are all the more able to make vital contributions to resource management and conservation. So on this front too there is need for a radical reorientation of development policies in order to upgrade the status of women.[199]

POLICY ANALYSIS AND RESEARCH

Despite the central significance of research on sustainable development, there has been all too little assessment of the multiple linkages between population factors and environmental degradation with a view to evaluating their dynamic interactions.[16,356-360] We lack even basic models to formulate significant linkages backed by comprehensive empirical data.

There is little argument, however, about the need to undertake the research. As early as 1984, the World Bank recognized the importance of population growth and other factors in overall development objectives: "In short, policies to reduce population growth can make an important contribution to development (especially in the long-run), but their beneficial effects will be greatly diminished if they are not supported by the right macro-economic and sectoral policies. At the same time, failure to address the population problem will itself reduce the set of macro-economic and sectoral policies that are possible, and permanently foreclose some long-run development options."[360]

This research lacuna seems to have arisen because the scientific disciplines in question have traditionally been pursued in some isolation from each other, and through overly static rather than dynamic models. Understanding the linkages in question can only be achieved through analyses that are methodically integrative from the start – as integrative as workings in the real world. In other words, the emphasis should be on interdisciplinary studies, with focus on the multi-faceted feedbacks between supposedly discrete areas. The research will thus serve to illuminate the critical question of sustainable development in general; and, in particular, it will evaluate the contentious issue of population carrying capacity.

It should not be difficult in principle to mount a research programme of sufficient scope to cope. But in practice, it will mark a solid departure from the often limited, uncoordinated and *ad hoc* endeavours to date. A target date for completion should be the June 1992 United Nations Conference on Environment and Development.

POPULATION POLICIES FOR DEVELOPED NATIONS

Finally, let us review the scope for population policies in developed countries. This option is rarely considered; indeed, it is hardly ever perceived as a worthwhile option at all. Not a single such country has indicated it wishes to reduce its population growth rate. But because the consumerist patterns of developed nations induce much environmental degradation, especially as regards ozone-layer depletion and global warming, and because these threats reflect (in part at least) the continuing population growth of developed nations, the question deserves brief assessment here.

There is some ostensible justification for the lack of population policies on the part of developed nations. Their average population growth rate is 0.5 per cent a year, by comparison with a developing-world average of 2.1 per cent. Developed-world populations now total 1.2 billion people, or 23 per cent of the global total. They are projected to grow by only 52 million (4 per cent) by the year 2000, whereas developing-world populations are projected to grow by 824 million (20 per cent). The respective figures for 2020 are 130 million (11 per cent) and 2.6 billion (62 per cent). So is not the main population growth problem confined to developing nations? That depends on how one assesses the repercussions of population growth.

As we have seen in Chapter 1, it is necessary to consider the entire impact of population growth on the planetary natural resource base that ultimately sustains all human societies. This can be undertaken in accord with the basic analytic equation I = PAT (see *Critical Linkages* in Chapter 1), which reflects population in multiplicative relationship with affluence and technology. What, then, is the environmental impact of an "average" American, Canadian or Japanese, who consumes, according to a recent reckoning,[25] up to 50 times more environmentally-based goods and services per capita than does an average Chinese? To feed each American requires at least 1,500 kilograms of agricultural products, a Chinese less than 600 kilograms, or only 40 per cent as much – with all that implies for increased pressures on agricultural land.[361] Furthermore, an average American consumes 8,000 litres of fossil fuel (oil equivalent), a Chinese just over 400 litres, or only 5 per cent as much – with all that implies for global climate change.

So it is relevant for governments of developed countries to ask themselves how many citizens constitute a sustainable total for their countries, and for the world community too. Of course, the environmental impact of developed countries' lifestyles is a function of their consumerism and technologies too, and there is much scope to alleviate the impact through corrective action in these spheres as well as in the population field. But the population component remains an integral part of the I = PAT equation. Hence, it is significant in developed countries as well.

CRITICAL POLICY OPTIONS: A SUMMARY

Despite the progress made over the past two decades to tackle the problems posed by rapid population growth and uneven distribution, rampant urbanization, high fertility levels, and poor access to family planning and maternal and child health care services (among other factors), much remains to be done. Coordinated action is needed at all levels – international, national and local. Population and environment issues overlap at many intersections, but the following policy recommendations are essential not only for securing improvements in quality of life and environmental management, but for reaching a sustainable future.

International action
• Institutional links and coordination mechanisms should be set up between international organizations – United Nations agencies, non-governmental organizations, scientific and academic institutions – dealing with aspects of global environmental problems and population issues. It is necessary to take a coordinated approach to development over the next decade. Piecemeal solutions will clearly not suffice.
• More funding should be made available for research and analysis of the important linkages between population and global environmental issues, such as climate change, ozone-layer depletion, sea level rise, and changes in biogeochemical cycles.
• There should be more cooperation and coordination of activities among donor countries and organizations working in the field of

environment and population.
• More efforts need to be devoted to raising the awareness of policy makers, planners and economists to the necessity of taking a coordinated approach to the problems of population growth, distribution, urbanization and other related issues and resource degradation.

National action
• Establish mechanisms for coordinating programmes dealing with population and resource issues.
• Support research concerning the major links between population and the environment.
• Incorporate population concerns into National Conservation Strategies.
• Prepare country profiles focusing on the interaction between poverty, population and the environment.
• Support studies on "population supporting capacities" of key resources: agricultural lands, forests, water supplies, grasslands and coastal zones.
• Identify vulnerable eco-zones – arid lands, smallholder agricultural areas, vulnerable uplands, tropical forests, coastal areas, etc., – where the double pressures of rapid population growth and over-exploitation of natural resources create serious problems.
• Introduce coordinated government-backed action programmes to improve conditions in vulnerable eco-zones.
• Identify appropriate non-governmental organizations capable of participating in national conservation and population programmes and other environment-population oriented activities.
• Support action programmes to promote and improve women's education levels, health status, employment opportunities, and participation in national and local decision-making. Include status of women in national development plans.
• Support research and data collection on population distribution, urbanization trends, internal migration patterns and natural resource use.
• Incorporate population-environment concepts in both formal and non-formal educational systems.

Local action
• Establish cooperation and coordination between local and national officials, and among local officials, community groups and non-governmental organizations, for the planning and implementation of

environment-population projects.

• Encourage community participation in identifying problems and formulating solutions to locally-perceived population and environment problems.

• Assess success stories with the view of transplanting key elements to other projects.

• Identify local non-governmental organizations capable of participating in population-environment projects.

• Promote integrated community development studies and projects to include environmental conservation, maternal and child health care and family planning and women's issues.

• Encourage the participation of women in all development activities.

• Promote awareness creation at the local level through the creation of community development or conservation committees, the formation of mothers' groups, and the designation of village health and family planning motivators.

Most of these recommendations should be carried out anyway for reasons of sound economic development. They are more compelling when set within the context of the immense population and resource challenges facing humanity over the course of the decisive decade of the 1990s and beyond. Time is not on our side. Action is needed now. It cannot come soon enough.

CONCLUSION

According to Dr. Nafis Sadik, Executive Director of the United Nations Population Fund, "The next 10 years will decide the shape of the 21st century. They may decide the future of the Earth as a habitation for humans."[1] Environmental decline has become so widespread and significant that the World Commission on Environment and Development described it as a threat second only to nuclear war.[2] And that statement applied to a 1987 world with 5 billion people. Within the next half century we must anticipate a projected world population of nearly twice as many people, seeking three times as much food and fibre and perhaps four times as much energy, and engaging in five to 10 times as much economic activity – with all the environmental stresses that will likely entrain.

How far population pressures constitute a determining factor in today's environmental decline – and how much environmental decline contributes to population pressures – is important but perhaps not as important as deciding on an action agenda and relevant policies to correct population and environment problems that will only become more deeply entrenched with time. The recommendations and policy directives presented here constitute a beginning. They need refinement, the benefit of more experience and wisdom at the regional, national and local level, and far more extensive funding. Humankind can still build a "common future", if sufficient action is taken by enough countries in enough time to make a real difference.

APPENDIX I

STATEMENT ON POPULATION AND ENVIRONMENT

UNFPA: MEETING ON POPULATION AND ENVIRONMENT, 4-5 MARCH, 1991

Preamble

In December, 1987, General Assembly Resolution 42/186 welcomed "... the aspirational goals to the year 2000 and beyond as set out in The Environmental Perspective, namely: Achievement over time of such a balance between population and environmental capacities as would make possible sustainable development, keeping in view the links among population levels, consumption patterns, poverty and the natural resource base." [Paragraph 4, and sub-item "a"; adopted on the basis of the report "The Environmental Perspective to the Year 2000" of the Second Committee.]

Subsequently, in August, 1990, the first Preparatory Committee Meeting of the 1992 United Nations Conference on Environment and Development requested the Secretary-General of the United Nations Conference on Environment and Development "... to submit to the Preparatory Committee at its second session a progress report underlining the close interrelationship between development and environment... as well as of, inter alia, *the following elements... The relationship between demographic pressures and unsustainable consumption patterns and environmental degradation."*

And in December, 1990, General Assembly Resolution 45/216 further "Emphasizes the importance of addressing the relationship between demographic pressures and unsustainable consumption patterns and environmental degradation during the preparatory process of the United Nations Conference on Environment and Development, taking into account the subsequent decisions of the Preparatory Committee for the United Nations Conference on Environment and Development, in accordance with General Assembly resolution 44/228 of 22 December 1989."

It is in the context of the above, that the United Nations Population Fund sponsored a special meeting on population and environment at which participants agreed, by consensus, to the following statement. [The meeting was held at UNFPA Headquarters, 4-5 March 1991; a list of participants is attached.]

Introduction

Over the past 20 years, since the Stockholm Conference on the Human Environment, development has progressed unevenly throughout the world, poverty has deepened in many areas, women's status has not improved significantly, and environments have become increasingly degraded. During this period, world population grew from approximately 3.7 billion in 1970 to over 5.3 billion today. Now, as plans are being laid for the United Nations Conference on Environment and Development in 1992, the population of the world is currently growing by 250,000 each day and the United Nations forecasts that upwards of another 2 billion people will be placing demands on

119

the planet's finite resources in the short span of just two decades.

Population size, growth and spatial distribution can impact on environment and sustainable development in multiple ways, and environmental outcomes have important implications for the well-being of populations as well. As world population grows to historically unknown levels, and as the pace of urbanization continues unabated, resource depleting technologies, lifestyles that generate excessive wastes, and economic practices that are often at odds with environmental conservation and sustainable development are likely to exert unprecedented effects on our atmosphere, lands and forests, mineral and energy resources, oceans and quality of life.

Meeting the challenge of population size, change and imbalances in distribution, in the context of continued degradation of critical resources – forests, soils, air, water, fauna and flora – is therefore one of the most important tasks facing humankind. Indeed, recognizing the interconnectedness of environmental protection, economic development and population trends has become a crucial challenge for world leaders. Fortunately, there is much to be gleaned from positive initiatives in the past – initiatives at the local, national, regional and international level which represent a rich repository of pathways to help correct imbalances in the relationship between population and natural resources, thus fostering sustainable development in the process.

In many cases, the key issue is time – time needed by governments of all countries to adapt and innovate environmentally conscious technologies; to carefully manage and protect fragile ecosystems and regenerate degraded lands; to build up their capital resources, invest in infrastructure, and service debts. Time is also needed to insure basic needs and fulfilment of human rights through improved health and nutritional services, eradication of illiteracy, and empowerment of women as managers of both environment and reproduction.

In spite of past initiatives, the seriousness of the environmental problems demands a new approach. Policy analysis, planning and accounting practices simply cannot ignore the fact that the world's stock of natural resources is finite; even the regenerative capability of renewable resources is limited and this is becoming even more critical with population growth. Take the quantity and quality of freshwater as an example. Only around 3 per cent of the total amount of water on Earth is freshwater and of this amount, only a tenth of 1 per cent can be utilized by society. Already, many arid areas in the Middle East, Africa and parts of Asia are suffering severe water shortages – a problem that will grow worse as populations continue to expand in these water deficit regions. Thus, today, many countries face severe water constraints, hampering efforts at improving their economies.

Sustainable development implies that national development strategies balance population with available resources. Within such a framework of sustainable use, "resource security" then becomes a possibility. Countries and regions no longer need fear they are pushing the red line of resource use. Strategic planning for human needs and resource management to meet those needs are therefore two fundamental components of sustainable development. But planning and resource management may well fail unless development plans are integrated in such a way that population dynamics are included in resource assessments. It is fundamental that population and resource issues be seen together from a new perspective.

Identification of priority environmental problems

Human activities and population dynamics are inextricably connected to environmental problems in all countries. In developing countries, for example, where great demographic pressure is being brought upon the natural resource base, priority areas stand out. Consider the following:

• Problems of soil erosion and desertification, linked with inappropriate land use practices often brought on by migration patterns.

• Problems of environmental degradation derived from deforestation resulting from inappropriate shifting cultivation patterns, fuelwood demands, and conversion of forests in uplands areas to other uses, linked with demographic pressures among poorest groups, movements of population into marginal areas, and environmental refugees.

• Problems of water scarcity, misuse and pollution of water resources in both rural and urban areas, linked with the effects of demographic momentum and spatial concentrations of population in and around congested towns and cities.

• The impact of changes in land use and agricultural practices – particularly slash-and-burn practices – on production of greenhouse gases, linked with expanding populations and their needs in the African savannah, Amazonia and many areas in Asia.

• The immense challenge of providing basic services in the face of rapid urbanization and industrialization, as well as the unplanned squatter settlements that proliferate in and around major urban areas.

• The challenge of managing coastal areas where populations are growing rapidly and critical resources are being depleted at an accelerated rate – such as in highly urbanized coastal areas.

In developed countries, where high rates of consumption are evident, priority areas may stand out clearly as when population demands for goods and services promote inappropriate economic activity, resulting in substantial release of greenhouse gases, ozone-depleting substances, nitrogen oxides, and other pollutants; the proliferation of municipal and toxic wastes; and increasing pollution of coastal areas and regional seas.

Identification of such problems may be facilitated at the local level by drawing upon expertise to earmark "ecologically endangered zones", for example, where high population densities prevail – such as forested uplands, coastal fishing areas, smallholder agriculture in lowland areas, arid grazing lands, tropical forests, and urban slums. In other instances, more sophisticated environmental monitoring and evaluation mechanisms may be needed at the national, regional and even international level in cases where problems exacerbated by imbalances in population growth and distribution escape more direct forms of detection such as pollutants in water supplies, or release of greenhouse gases.

Identification of key population groups who may be agents of environmental conservation or most vulnerable to degradation

Substantial effort is now needed to identify key population groups who may be especially vulnerable to environmental degradation, and those with special potential to act as agents of environmental conservation. Key population subgroups needing priority attention tend to be poor households; those in rural settings including landless and smallholder households are particularly vulnerable. In urban settings, the same often applies to households in squatter settlements. Populations in low-lying deltaic zones, and those living close to coasts protected by coral reefs are especially vulnerable to sea level rise and destruction of coral communities which buffer wave action and protect coastlines from storm surges. Gender considerations are of central importance. Women play pivotal roles in assuring food security and good nutrition practices, fuelwood supplies, and clean water, among other things.

Equally important is to consider demographic correlates of the world's "bottom billion" people – those pressured into unsustainable use of resources due to poverty and survival needs. As population growth rates tend to be relatively high among poorest families – those with limited income, education, access to health facilities – national environmental strategies should also consider effects of higher child dependency ratios, needs of migrant households and environmental refugees on the carrying capacity of local ecologies. Special consideration should be given to the fiscal capacity of local governments to accommodate basic social and economic needs.

On the other hand, in the case of the world's "top billion", demographic patterns should also be assessed in developing national environmental strategies. Internal migration, changing household size, extended life expectancy and growing shares of the elderly will also have major environmental consequences in terms of changed residential and consumption patterns.

Just as those who are most vulnerable are in need of technical assistance to help facilitate improved productive and conservation practices, they also tend to be in greatest need of primary health care and family planning services. Moreover, populations in high-consuming countries may have special potential for acting as agents of environmental conservation by increasing the efficiency of their energy and resource use.

Another group of people who play key roles as resource managers, but are also among the most vulnerable to resource degradation, are indigenous ethnic peoples. Worldwide, about 200 million people belong to indigenous cultures. Many rainforest people in the Americas, Africa, and Southeast Asia have lived in harmony with their environments for centuries. Increasingly, such groups are coming under intense pressures from landless migrants and governments intent on developing "under-utilized land".

Integration of population considerations in national environmental strategies and national development plans

National capacities in policy analysis and planning, identification of ecologically endangered zones, and identification of key population groups can be translated into action in the form of **national environment strategies** and **national development plans.** Special emphasis should be placed on those plans and policies that achieve multiple objectives, encouraging sustainable economic development and minimizing long-term environmental damage.

Such endeavours should go far beyond simple projections of population growth patterns (in a separate chapter of a National Development Plan, for example). They should consider the short and long-term effects of absolute population size as well as population growth rates and distribution patterns. The effects of such growth on specific environmental sectors as well as on specific producing and service sectors in the economy – including demands for socio-economic infrastructure, land and food supplies, housing and space – have important environment and resource use implications. In some cases, the implications of projects over the short-run will be of utmost interest, especially in countries where population may double in the brief span of only 20 to 30 years. In other cases, long-run sustainability will be of interest as gradual changes in population size and distribution alter resource use and consumption.

Another important factor is the effect of "population momentum" as it relates to growth of the working-age population, demands for employment growth, and possible impacts of an expanded employment base on natural resource use and sustainability. Integration of population considerations should further consider environmental implications of population distribution patterns – not only global patterns but also within countries and how they affect urban and rural sectors.

Planning should take into consideration gender selectivity in the use and management of key resources. Women not only depend on resources, but in many areas resources depend on women. In a significant number of developing countries, women act as *de facto* environmental managers. But too often policies and programmes ignore them. Investing in women – particularly in terms of education and training – contributes to women's status, the building of a more skilled workforce, helps achieve a sustainable demographic equilibrium, and improves environmental management where it is most needed, on the ground.

National capacity building
A fundamental objective is to help nations develop the capacity to assess the implications of current and projected population growth and distribution patterns, and their potential impact on use of natural resources and sustainable development. This applies to both developed and developing countries alike. To be effective, national environment strategies require information on population parameters – size, growth, spatial distribution, short and long-run dynamics – at the local as well as the national level. In addition, as environmental problems often extend beyond national borders, governments should assess the implications of their behaviour for the global commons as well, such as seas and the atmosphere.

This can be facilitated through improved policy analysis, research, data collection and national development planning which integrates population

planning into environment and development planning. Key facets of this process include the following:
- Awareness creation activities, such as seminars for policy makers. A critical part of awareness creation is consideration of the cultural, moral and ethical dimensions of sustainability at varying levels of population and technological adaptation.
- Carefully targeted training programmes to upgrade national skills in population and environmental planning.
- Longer-term population education as regards the inter-locking relationships between population and environment, in the formal and non-formal educational sector.
- Incorporation of the concept of population supporting potential and the environment as a dynamic and powerful component of the planning process; with appropriate moral and ethical considerations, the latter to be judiciously adapted in the context of local, national and global activities.

National capacity building will be improved by coordination between major players in the population, economic and environmental sectors: industry, research institutes, non-governmental organizations, universities, and government agencies. The development of better integrative forecasting methodologies at the international and national level would not only enhance our understanding of the critical links between population, resources and the environment, but would also contribute to interdisciplinary problem solving and better cooperation between key sectors. Of great importance in this context is to optimize complementarities in policies and activities that can benefit the environment and encourage sustainable development, while simultaneously identifying and correcting non-complementary policies that can produce negative, unintended effects.

Regional and international concerns affecting the global commons

Environmental problems do not respect national borders. The effects of environmental degradation in any one country often impact on its neighbours as well as on the global commons. Demographic pressures resulting in desertification, deforestation, loss of freshwater and coastal resources, and air and water pollution are some examples of this trend. All governments must therefore collaborate on assessing how local level problems produce regional and global effects, and the kinds of action needed at the regional and global level to tackle the root causes. Such collaboration will be particularly important for relatively poor countries, given shortages of resources to meet basic needs let alone to import cleaner technologies. Such collaboration involving more developed countries will also be essential as their relatively large impacts on the global commons will have immense spillover effects for poorer countries – for example through sea-level rise, atmospheric pollution and ocean pollution.

Challenge to policy makers

Perhaps there is no time in humanity's past when so much attention and creative energy will be devoted to safeguarding our future as during preparations up to, during and after the 1992 United Nations Conference on Environment and Development. A relationship between population and environment has been demonstrated in many cases, and it can be argued that the linkage between these two factors is fundamental.

Many of the issues to be faced are daunting and undeniably complex. At the heart of each issue is human activity – not only what we produce and consume or how we do it – but numbers of people that exist today as well as those expected in the future; how they will be distributed in rural areas, towns and cities; and how the relationship between population and natural resources can be balanced to contribute more effectively to sustainable development.

While no one can pretend to have all the answers to these questions, one thing is clear – it is vital that we assess, monitor and evaluate the problems involved and try to identify constructive ways to solve them at the national and international level. It is the capacity of humans to plan their future – their ecological, economic, and demographic future – that distinguishes them from other species. And it is on the occasion of the 1992 United Nations Conference on Environment and Development that real progress in planning for more optimal relationships between population and environment can be set in motion.

As emphasized in this statement, the ingredients of imaginative policy and planning in the area of population and environment can begin with development of national capacities whereby governments can better institute their own mechanisms to assess and plan for sustainable populations and natural resource use. Cooperation between international agencies and non-governmental organizations can further help to facilitate this process by sharing methodologies and analytical frameworks for monitoring and evaluating the problems involved; by providing training in the skills needed to integrate population issues in national environment strategies; and through joint ventures whereby complex inter-sectoral facets of environment and population problems are tackled by the shared expertise of several environment and development agents.

And, finally, it is prudent to acknowledge there is much wisdom that is available to build upon. The idea of integrated population, environment and sustainable development projects is not new – a great many success stories exist in a growing number of countries. Insofar as population growth is an important element of the problem, we know that more optimal outcomes can be achieved with investments in data collection and analysis, primary health care, women's education, fulfilment of unmet needs in family planning services, strategies for more balanced spatial distribution and urban development, and inter-sectoral programmes with complementary social, economic and ecological components. The real success story, however, will be contingent on whether far more effort and initiative is achieved in this critical area, and urgently, in face of an ever growing constraint – a limited amount of time in which to respond effectively to the unparalleled challenges ahead.

LIST OF PARTICIPANTS *

United Nations Population Fund Sponsored Meeting on Population and Environment, March 4-5, 1991, UNFPA Headquarters, New York

Experts

Mr. George Benneh
Chairman, Department of Geography
and Resource Development, and
Director, Population Impact Project
University of Ghana
PO Box 59
Legon, Ghana

Mr. Gerardo Budowski
University for Peace
Director, Natural Resources
Apartado 198, 2300 Curridabat
San José, Costa Rica

Ms. Nazli Choucri
Professor of Political Science
Dept of Political Science
Massachusetts Institute of Technology
Cambridge, MA 02139

Ms. Martine Coursil
United Nations Environment
Programme
DC2-8th Floor
New York, NY 10017

Ms. Maria Concepcion J. Cruz
Professor
Institute of Environmental Science
and Management
University of the Philippines
Los Banos, Philippines

Mr. Nibhon Debavalya
Chief, Population Division, ESCAP
Bangkok, Thailand

Mr. Sofian Effendi
Director, Population Studies Center
Gadjah Mada University
Bulaksumur G-7,
Yogyakarta 55281, Indonesia

Ms. Julia Gardner
School of Community and
Regional Planning
University of British Columbia
Vancouver, V6T 1W5
British Columbia, Canada

Mr. Serguey Ivanov
Population and Development Unit
United Nations, Room DC 2-2040
New York, NY 10017

Ms. Anna-Liisa Korhonen
Deputy Director General
FINNIDA, Ministry of Foreign Affairs
Helsinki, Finland

Ms. Louise Lassonde
Population Advisor
United Nations Conference on
Environment and Development
160 Route de Florissant
PO Box 80
CH-1231 Conches
Geneva, Switzerland

Mr. Alfonso Mata
Director, Tropical Science Center
Apartado Postal B-3870
1000 San José, Costa Rica

Mr. Irving Mintzer
9514 Garwood St.
Silverspring, Maryland 20901

Mr. Hani Mulki
President, Royal Scientific Society
P.O. Box 6945
Amman, Jordan

Mr. Gayle Ness
Professor of Sociology
University of Michigan
Ann Arbor, MI

Mr. Robert J. Nicholls
Research Scholar
Laboratory for Coastal Research
Department of Geography
University of Maryland
College Park, Maryland 20742
(visiting from UK)

Ms. Maureen O'Neil
Executive Director
North-South Institute
200-55 Murray Street , 2nd Floor
Ottawa, Ontario, K1N 5M3, Canada

Mr. G. M. Oza
General Secretary
International Society of Naturalists
(INSONA)
Oza Building
Salatwada, Baroda 390 001 India

Mr. J. Sadok
Senior Economist, Designate
United Nations Conference for
Environment and Development
Geneva, Switzerland

Mr. Mahendra Shah
8 Mentmore Close
Kenton, Harrow
Middlesex, HA3 OEA, United Kingdom

Mr. Mohamed Soerjani
University of Indonesia
Director of Centre for Research for Human
Resources and the Environment
Jalansalemba 4
Jakarta 10430, Indonesia

Mr. Georges P. Tapinos
Fondation Nationale des Sciences Politiques
Institut d'Etudes Politiques de Paris
27 Rue Saint-Guillaume
75341 Paris cedex 07, France

Mr. Sufyan Tell
Director, Environment Protection
Government
Amman, Jordan

Ms. Pietronella van den Oever
World Conservation Union
Ave. du Mont-Blanc
CH-1196 Gland, Switzerland

Mr. Paul J. Werbos
Program Director
National Science Foundation
1800 G Street, NW
Washington, DC 20550

Ms. Nancy Yates
Women and Environment Unit
United Nations Development
Programme
New York, NY 10017

NGO observers

Mr. Werner Fornos
President, Population Institute
110 Maryland Ave., NE
Washington, DC 30002

Mr. Carl Gaywell
Zero Population Growth
1400 16th St. NW
Suite 320
Washington, DC 20036

Ms. Sunetra Puri
International Planned
Parenthood Federation
Regent's College
Inner Circle, Regent's Park
London, NW1 4NS, United Kingdom

Mr. George Zeidenstein
President, Population Council
1 Dag Hammarskjold Plaza
New York, NY 10017

* Note: Participants attended the Meeting in their individual capacities, not as official spokespersons for their governments or other agencies.

KEY RESOLUTIONS AND STATEMENTS ON POPULATION AND ENVIRONMENT

REPORT OF THE WORLD COMMISSION ON ENVIRONMENT AND DEVELOPMENT (1987)

Rapidly growing populations can increase the pressure on resources and slow any rise in living standards; thus sustainable development can only be pursued if population size and growth are in harmony with the changing productive potential of the ecosystem. *(p.9)*

In many parts of the world, population is growing at rates that cannot be sustained by available environmental resources, at rates that are outstripping any reasonable expectations of improvements in housing, health care, food security, or energy supplies. *(p.11)*

Governments that need to should develop long-term, multi-faceted population policies and campaigns to pursue broad demographic goals... *(p.11)*

FIRST AFRICAN REGIONAL CONFERENCE ON ENVIRONMENT AND SUSTAINABLE DEVELOPMENT

The Kampala Declaration on Sustainable Development in Africa, June 1989

Our countries are already confronted by many problems of environmental pollution and depletion of natural resources resulting from our own national as well as international policies and pressures... In the context of reviving economic growth with greater equity and meeting the essential needs for food, water, energy and jobs for our people, we resolve to take immediate action on the following priority issues and goals for achieving sustainable development in our countries and continent:

– Managing demographic change and pressures.
– Achieving food self-sufficiency and food security.
– Ensuring efficient and equitable use of water resources.
– Securing greater energy self-sufficiency.
– Optimizing industrial production.
– Maintaining species and ecosystems.
– Preventing and reversing desertification.

(paragraphs 1 and 6)

INTERNATIONAL FORUM ON POPULATION IN THE TWENTY-FIRST CENTURY

The Amsterdam Declaration, November 1989

We the participants of the International Forum on Population in the Twenty-first Century ...

– **Acknowledge** that population, resources and environment are inextricably linked and stress our commitment to bringing about a sustainable relationship between human numbers, resources and development.

– **Express concern** that the continued rapid growth in world population, especially in the developing world, the processes of uncontrolled migration and urbanization and the increasing degradation of environment everywhere threaten to darken our vision of the world we will leave for posterity in the twenty-first century. *(paragraph 1)*

The implications of such developments are staggering. Nearly everywhere increasing demands are damaging the natural resource base – land, water and air – upon which all life depends. Moreover, poverty is widespread and growing: For some 1.2 billion people, poverty is a way of life. *(paragraph 6)*

Clearly, it is a time for concerted action. The triad of population growth and distribution, environmental degradation and pervasive poverty threatens us and our planet as never before. Future generations must be given the opportunity to live in fair and just societies, enjoy basic human rights and have equal access to all the benefits society has to offer. *(paragraph 7)*

The Forum participants further call on: All countries

– To adopt integrated population, environmental and natural resource management policies, including those which address population movement and distribution with the objective of minimizing their negative consequences.

– To ensure that the results and follow-up of this Forum are duly taken into account in the formulation of the international development strategy for the fourth United Nations Development Decade as well as in the preparations for and the deliberations of the 1992 United Nations Conference on Environment and Development... *(paragraph 21)*

STATEMENT ON POPULATION STABILIZATION BY WORLD LEADERS

Mankind has many challenges: to obtain a lasting peace between nations; to preserve the quality of the environment; to conserve natural resources at a sustainable level; to advance the economic and social progress of the less developed nations; and to stabilize population growth.

Degradation of the world's environment, income inequality, and the potential for conflict exist today because of over-consumption and over-population. If this unprecedented population growth continues, future generations of children will not have adequate food, housing, medical care, education, earth resources, and employment opportunities.

Recognizing that early population stabilization is in the interest of all nations, we earnestly hope that leaders around the world will share our views and join with us in this great undertaking for the well-being and happiness of people everywhere.

Signed by leaders of the following countries:

Austria	Haiti	Panama
Bangladesh	Iceland	Philippines
Barbados	India	Rwanda
Bhutan	Indonesia	Senegal
Botswana	Jamaica	Seychelles
Cape Verde	Japan	Singapore
China	Jordan	Sri Lanka
Colombia	Kenya	St. Kitts-Nevis
Cyprus	Republic of Korea	St. Lucia
Dominica	Liberia	St. Vincent and the Grenadines
Dominican Republic	Malta	Sudan
Egypt	Mauritius	Thailand
Fiji	Morocco	Tunisia
Grenada	Nepal	Vanuatu
Guinea-Bissau	Nigeria	Zimbabwe

(Organized by Population Communication, November, 1989)

ASIAN WOMEN PARLIAMENTARIANS' CONFERENCE ON POPULATION AND THE STATUS OF WOMEN, MARCH 1990

We, Parliamentarians from 26 countries of Asia... hereby declare the following principles:
– Sustainable development means creating a balance between population growth and the environment in order to ensure the future of coming generations. *(paragraph 3)*
– The inextricable link between population and the status of women, if reflected in socio-economic policies, including family planning programmes, will help eliminate poverty, achieve sustainable development and promote stability and peace. *(paragraph 6)*

GENERAL ASSEMBLY OF ASIAN FORUM OF PARLIAMENTARIANS

Third General Assembly on Population and Development, October 1990

We, the Parliamentarians from 21 countries of Asia
– **Recognize** that the further integration of population concerns into development planning is essential to the stabilization of population growth

rates in all countries of Asia, which in turn is critical to our collective efforts to balance population, resources and the environment and to sustain development. *(paragraph 1)*

Increasing human demands are damaging the natural resource base – land, water and air – upon which all development depends. Population plays a key role in this process. For any given type of technology, level of consumption or waste, level of poverty or equality, the more people there are, the greater is the impact on the environment. This is particularly true of the degradation of the soils and forests of developing countries and global warming, both of which currently pose the greatest threat to human welfare and survival. Establishing a sustainable relationship between human numbers and resources in the Asian context will require, among other things: *(from paragraph 8)*

– Slowing and actively stabilizing population growth.
– Providing suitable directions and measures for balanced urban development.
– Adopting legislation to protect village forest and farmland rights, particularly those of the poorest farmers and women.
– Investing in the agricultural resource base, both to enhance the productivity of existing farmland and to rehabilitate and revitalize degraded agricultural land.
– Ensuring the adequate supply and timely distribution of food to all sectors of society especially the underprivileged groups.
– Prohibiting the use of environmentally unsafe fertilizers and pesticides; and dumping of industrial wastes.
– Promulgating appropriate laws to prevent deforestation.
– Developing and introducing environmentally safe industrial processes.
– Educating and encouraging farmers in better water and irrigation management and in the use of land.

MINISTERIAL DECLARATION OF THE SECOND WORLD CLIMATE CONFERENCE, NOVEMBER 1990

We **urge** that special attention be given to the economic and social dimensions of climate and climate change research...

The measures adopted should take into account different socio-economic contexts... We **note** that per capita consumption patterns in certain parts of the world along with a projected increase in world population are contributing factors in the projected increase in greenhouse gases. *(from paragraphs 6, 7 and 9)*

IUCN-THE WORLD CONSERVATION UNION

General Assembly of IUCN-The World Conservation Union, 18th Session, Perth, Australia, December 1990

Urges member governments, and other members of IUCN, and the Director General to use their best efforts to ensure that population issues are given high priority at the 1992 United Nations Conference on Environment and Development; and that environmental issues, including human life support systems, are given equivalent prominence at the 1994 United Nations International Population Conference.

Encourages IUCN members and the IUCN Secretariat to continue to take the lead in exploring and initiating actions on the relations between:

A. population growth and distribution, finite natural resources and attainable quality of life;

B. human population trends and the survival of other species;

C. family size, changes in social and cultural behaviour and technologies and patterns of resource use;

D. natural resource management and human health, particularly the morbidity and mortality of infants and young children;

E. over-consumption, urbanization, rural impoverishment and options for sustainable resource use and management;

F. women in development and their role in the process of achieving environmental sustainability.

Requests the Director General and Secretariat, in advising governments on the formulation and implementation of National Conservation Strategies, to take all appropriate steps to ensure that the population characteristics of a country, including growth, distribution, urbanization, age-sex structure, family size, morbidity, mortality, migration and labour force structure are integrated in the planning process, and that population-related resource stress is analyzed not only from the point of view of sustainable use and management but also the quality of human life as defined in the Universal Declaration of Human Rights, and the World Health Organization's definition of health. *(Section 18.17; paragraphs 1, 3 and 4)*

REPORT OF THE SOUTH COMMISSION

We are greatly concerned that the population in many countries of the South is growing at an explosive and, in the long run, unsustainable pace. The present high rates of population growth increase the burden of dependency and reduce the resources available for raising productivity to what is sufficient just to maintain subsistence levels. In several countries, the pressure of growing numbers on the limited fertile land is accelerating the degradation of land and water resources and causing excessive deforestation. Rapid population growth is also a principal factor in the uncontrolled growth of vast urban agglomerations. In many large cities of the South, islands of affluence are surrounded by sprawling slums in which the evils of poor housing, polluted air and water, bad sanitation, and widespread disease are compounded by the activities of drug peddlers, smugglers, and other undesirable elements.

In the long run the problem of overpopulation of the countries of the South can be fully resolved only through their development. But action to contain the rise of population cannot be postponed. The present trends in population, if not moderated, have frightening implications for the ability of the South to meet the twin challenges of development and environmental security in the twenty-first century.

It takes time before even well-designed policies can have a material impact on the birth rate. It is therefore necessary that countries with high birth rates should act without delay and adopt policies which will have an impact on population growth in a reasonable period of time. *(pages 279-80)*

Countries represented by members of the South Commission:

Algeria	Mexico
Argentina	Mozambique
Brazil	Nigeria
China	Pakistan
Côte d'Ivoire	Philippines
Cuba	Senegal
Egypt	Sri Lanka
Guyana	Uruguay
India	Venezuela
Indonesia	Yugoslavia
Jamaica	Western Samoa
Kuwait	Zimbabwe
Malaysia	

(Chairman: Julius K. Nyerere, Tanzania: *The Challenge to the South: Report of the South Commission*, published by Oxford University Press, 1990.)

APPENDIX III SELECTED POPULATION CHARACTERISTICS : REGIONS AND COUNTRIES

	Population (thousands) 1990	Growth Rate (percent) 1990-95	Urban Population (percent) 1990-95	Doubling Time (years)	Population (thousands) 2020	Total Fertility Rate 1990-95	Contraceptive Prevalence Rate **	Government Agency for Pop. Policy 1988	Policy on Population Growth 1988	Policy Towards Fertility 1988	Policy on Contraceptive Use 1988	Policy on Internal Migration 1988
WORLD TOTAL	**5292195**	**1.73**	**45**	**40**	**8091628**	**3.31**	**51**					
LESS DEVELOPED REGIONS	**4085638**	**2.08**	**37**	**34**	**6749581**	**3.71**	**45**					
MORE DEVELOPED REGIONS	**1206556**	**0.48**	**73**	**146**	**1342048**	**1.88**	**70**					
AFRICA	**642111**	**3.02**	**34**	**23**	**1452067**	**6.03**	**14**					
WESTERN AFRICA	**193702**	**3.21**	**33**	**22**	**460383**	**6.66**	**na**					
Benin	4630	3.15	33	22	11369	7.11	9.2	2	4	4	3	4
Burkina Faso	8996	2.89	9	24	21327	6.50	na	1	4	3	4	4
Cape Verde	370	3.41	29	21	841	5.28	na	1	3	3	4	2
Côte d'Ivoire	11997	3.84	40	18	34776	7.41	2.9	1	1	1	3	2
Gambia	861	2.67	23	26	1736	6.17	na	1	3	3	4	3
Ghana	15028	3.17	33	22	32708	6.29	9.5	1	3	3	4	2
Guinea	5755	3.04	26	23	13820	7.00	na	1	4	4	4	4
Guinea-Bissau	964	2.14	20	33	1791	5.79	na	1	3	3	4	3
Liberia	2575	3.27	46	21	6477	6.70	6.4	1	3	3	4	3
Mali	9214	3.18	19	22	22439	7.11	4.6	1	2	2	4	2
Mauritania	2024	2.86	47	25	4642	6.50	0.8	2	4	3	3	2
Niger	7731	3.27	19	21	19406	7.11	na	2	3	3	4	4
Nigeria	108542	3.25	35	22	255393	6.60	4.8	1	3	3	4	2
Senegal	7327	2.79	38	25	15685	6.17	11.3	1	3	3	4	2
Sierra Leone	4151	2.65	32	26	9139	6.50	na	1	4	4	4	2
Togo	3531	3.18	26	22	8821	6.58	na	2	2	2	4	2
SOUTHERN AFRICA	**40928**	**2.32**	**55**	**30**	**74821**	**4.41**	**na**					
Botswana	1304	3.45	28	20	3095	6.39	27.8	2	3	3	4	2
Lesotho	1774	2.92	20	24	4013	5.79	5.3	2	3	3	4	4
South Africa	35282	2.18	59	32	61446	4.17	48.0	1	3	3	4	3
Swaziland	788	3.57	33	20	2023	6.50	na	2	3	3	4	4
NORTHERN AFRICA	**140553**	**2.50**	**45**	**28**	**256728**	**4.62**	**na**					
Algeria	24960	2.80	52	25	48484	4.86	na	1	3	3	4	2
Egypt	52426	2.15	47	32	85768	4.00	29.7	1	3	3	4	3

Libyan Arab Jamahiriya	4545	3.62	70	19	11567	6.66	na	2	4	4	2	2
Morocco	25061	2.43	48	29	43022	4.20	35.9	1	3	3	4	2
Sudan	25203	2.90	22	24	54627	6.26	4.6	2	4	4	4	2
Tunisia	8180	2.08	54	34	12925	3.38	41.1	1	3	3	4	3
MIDDLE AFRICA	**70054**	**3.13**	**38**	**22**	**172266**	**6.23**	**na**					
Angola	10020	2.81	28	25	22438	6.31	na	2	4	3	4	4
Cameroon	11833	3.42	41	20	32264	6.90	2.4	1	3	3	2	3
Central African Republic	3039	2.89	47	24	7154	6.19	na	2	4	4	4	3
Chad	5678	2.54	30	28	12013	5.79	na	2	4	4	3	4
Congo	2271	3.30	40	21	5860	6.29	na	2	4	4	4	2
Equatorial Guinea	352	2.55	29	27	752	5.89	na	1	1	1	2	3
Gabon	1172	3.30	46	21	2594	5.34	na	2	1	1	2	2
Sao Tome and Principe	121	2.27	na	31	219	na	na	2	2	2	4	2
Zaire	35568	3.24	39	22	88972	6.09	na	2	4	4	4	2
EASTERN AFRICA	**196873**	**3.30**	**22**	**21**	**487868**	**6.78**	**na**					
Burundi	5472	3.02	6	23	11950	6.79	8.7	1	3	3	4	1
Comoros	550	3.57	28	20	1510	7.03	na	1	3	3	4	2
Djibouti	409	2.95	81	24	979	6.50	na	2	4	4	2	3
Ethiopia	49240	2.98	13	24	114313	6.78	na	2	4	3	4	4
Kenya	24031	3.74	24	19	69799	6.80	17.0	1	3	3	4	3
Madagascar	12004	3.24	24	22	30272	6.50	na	1	4	4	3	3
Malawi	8754	3.63	12	19	22278	7.60	6.9	1	4	4	4	4
Mauritius	1082	1.08	40	65	1391	1.89	75.4	1	2	2	4	4
Mozambique	15656	2.70	27	26	32593	6.23	na	2	4	3	4	3
Rwanda	7237	3.46	8	20	17196	7.99	10.1	1	3	3	4	2
Seychelles	69	0.90	na	78	83	na	na	1	3	3	3	2
Somalia	7497	2.37	36	30	16905	6.60	na	1	4	4	4	3
Uganda	18794	3.75	10	19	48101	7.30	na	2	3	3	4	1
United Republic of Tanzania	27318	3.76	33	19	75485	7.11	na	1	4	4	4	3
Zambia	8452	3.80	50	18	23286	7.20	na	1	4	4	4	3
Zimbabwe	9709	3.11	28	23	20870	5.33	38.4	2	3	3	4	2
LATIN AMERICA AND CARIBBEAN	**448076**	**1.91**	**72**	**37**	**716294**	**3.25**	**56**					
SOUTH AMERICA	**296716**	**1.86**	**75**	**38**	**468004**	**3.21**	**na**					
Argentina	32322	1.17	86	60	43837	2.79	na	1	4	4	3	5
Bolivia	7314	2.82	51	25	16401	5.81	26.0	1	4	4	2	3

KEY

Government agency for population policy
1- Yes, 2- No, 9- Missing data

Government policy towards population growth
1- Raise, 2- Maintain, 3- Lower, 4- No intervention

Government policy towards fertility
1- Raise, 2- Maintain, 3- Lower, 4- No intervention

Policy on contraceptive use
1- Major limits (ML), 2- No ML: no support,
3- No ML: indirect support, 4- No ML: direct support

Government policy on internal migration
1- Accelerate trend, 2- Decelerate trend, 3- Reverse trend,
4- No intervention, 5- Maintain trend

Notes
*- Data not yet available for recently unified countries
**- Most recent data
na- Data not available

	Population (thousands) 1990	Growth Rate (percent) 1990-95	Urban Population (percent) 1990-95	Doubling Time (years)	Population (thousands) 2020	Total Fertility Rate 1990-95	Contraceptive Prevalence Rate **	Government Agency for Pop. Policy 1988	Policy on Population Growth 1988	Policy Towards Fertility 1988	Policy on Contraceptive Use 1988	Policy on Internal Migration 1988
Brazil	150368	1.87	75	37	233817	3.16	65.8	2	4	4	4	2
Chile	13173	1.55	86	45	18973	2.66	na	1	4	4	4	3
Colombia	32978	1.85	70	38	51520	2.92	64.8	2	4	3	4	2
Ecuador	10587	2.40	56	29	18706	3.87	44.3	1	3	3	4	3
Guyana	796	0.81	35	86	1111	2.40	31.4	2	4	4	4	3
Paraguay	4277	2.69	47	26	8423	4.34	44.8	2	4	4	3	2
Peru	21550	2.03	70	34	35390	3.57	45.8	1	3	3	4	2
Suriname	422	1.76	47	40	633	2.56	na	2	4	4	4	2
Uruguay	3094	0.58	85	120	3615	2.33	na	2	4	1	4	2
Venezuela	19735	2.37	90	30	35394	3.47	49.3	2	4	4	4	2
CENTRAL AMERICA	117676	2.19	66	32	200160	3.45	na					
Belize	187	2.16	na	32	299	na	na	2	4	4	3	2
Costa Rica	3015	2.25	47	31	4977	3.02	69.5	1	3	3	4	3
El Salvador	5252	2.47	44	28	10348	4.51	47.3	1	3	3	4	2
Guatemala	9197	2.88	39	24	19706	5.36	23.2	1	4	3	4	3
Honduras	5138	3.00	44	23	10558	4.94	34.9	1	3	3	2	2
Mexico	88598	2.01	73	35	142135	3.11	53.0	1	3	3	4	2
Nicaragua	3871	3.19	60	22	8435	5.01	27.0	1	3	3	4	3
Panama	2418	1.90	53	37	3702	2.87	58.2	1	4	4	4	3
CARIBBEAN	33685	1.40	60	50	48130	2.85	na					
Antigua and Barbuda	76	0.26	na	269	87	na	38.9	1	2	4	4	3
Bahamas	253	1.61	na	43	367	na	na	2	4	4	3	2
Barbados	255	0.31	45	227	293	1.79	46.5	1	3	2	4	4
Cuba	10608	0.89	75	79	12756	1.87	na	2	4	4	4	2
Dominica	82	0.61	na	115	100	na	49.0	2	3	3	4	4
Dominican Republic	7170	1.98	60	35	11001	3.34	50.0	1	3	3	4	3
Grenada	85	-0.35	na	-	87	na	31.0	2	3	3	4	2
Haiti	6513	2.05	28	34	12017	4.79	6.9	1	3	3	4	3
Jamaica	2456	1.17	52	60	3304	2.38	51.4	2	3	3	4	3
Saint Kitts and Nevis	44	0.04	na	1750	48	na	40.6	2	3	4	4	4
Saint Lucia	150	1.70	na	41	222	na	42.7	1	3	4	4	4
Saint Vincent and the Grenadines	116	1.04	na	67	152	na	41.5	1	3	3	4	3
Trinidad and Tobago	1281	1.42	69	49	1891	2.70	52.7	1	3	3	4	2

ASIA	3112695	1.84	34	38	4699827	3.26	50	2	4	4	4	4
SOUTHERN ASIA	1200569	2.28	27	31	2043908	4.44	na	1	4	3	3	4
Afghanistan	16557	6.68	18	10	37934	6.80	1.6	2	4	4	4	4
Bangladesh	115593	2.69	16	26	220119	5.13	25.2	1	3	3	4	1
Bhutan	1516	2.27	5	31	2861	5.54	na	1	4	4	4	2
India	853094	2.08	27	34	1371767	4.10	34.1	1	3	3	4	2
Iran, Islamic Republic of	54607	2.01	57	35	105966	4.70	na	1	4	4	4	2
Maldives	215	2.90	na	24	409	na	na	2	4	4	4	2
Nepal	19143	2.34	10	30	33080	5.54	13.9	1	3	3	4	2
Pakistan	122626	2.87	32	24	248116	5.95	7.6	1	3	4	4	2
Sri Lanka	17217	1.26	21	56	23656	2.47	62.0	1	3	4	4	5
SOUTH EASTERN ASIA	444767	1.94	30	36	690831	3.30	na	2	4	4	2	2
Brunei Darussalam	266	2.50	na	28	399	na	na	2	4	4	2	2
Democratic Kampuchea	8246	2.20	12	32	13266	4.41	na	2	1	1	4	3
Indonesia	184283	1.82	31	39	273349	3.10	47.9	1	3	3	4	2
Lao People's Democratic Republic	4139	2.92	19	24	8046	6.69	na	2	1	2	2	2
Malaysia	17891	2.27	43	31	28503	3.50	51.4	1	3	3	4	3
Myanmar	41675	2.09	25	33	68743	3.69	na	1	4	4	4	2
Philippines	62413	2.28	43	31	105384	3.91	45.3	1	3	3	4	3
Singapore	2723	1.08	100	65	3290	1.80	74.2	1	2	1	4	3
Thailand	55702	1.36	23	52	78118	2.20	67.5	1	3	3	4	4
Vietnam	66693	2.21	22	32	110638	3.70	na	1	3	3	4	3
EASTERN ASIA	1335605	1.31	40	53	1700741	2.19	na	1	3	4	4	5
China	1139060	1.42	33	49	1476852	2.25	74.0	1	4	4	4	3
Japan	123460	0.39	77	179	129029	1.70	64.3	2	1	2	4	2
Korea, Democratic People's Republic of	21773	1.92	60	36	31929	2.40	na	2	3	3	4	3
Korea, Republic of	42793	0.85	72	82	51178	1.65	70.4	1	3	3	4	3
Mongolia	2190	2.67	52	26	4423	4.70	na	2	2	3	1	2
WESTERN ASIA	131754	2.75	63	25	264347	4.74	na	2	4	4	2	4
Bahrain	516	3.08	83	23	943	3.69	na	2	4	1	3	3
Cyprus	701	0.90	53	78	874	2.23	na	1	1	3	3	2
Democratic Yemen*	2491	3.23	43	22	5801	6.48	na	1	4	3	4	2
Iraq	18920	3.39	71	21	45080	5.95	14.5	1	1	1	1	3
Israel	4600	1.50	92	47	6620	2.76	na	2	4	1	4	2
Jordan	4009	3.34	68	21	9042	5.54	26.5	1	4	4	4	4
Kuwait	2039	2.82	96	25	3593	3.45	na	1	2	1	1	2
Lebanon	2701	2.20	84	32	4446	3.38	53.0	2	4	4	4	2

KEY

Government agency for population policy
1- Yes, 2- No, 9- Missing data

Government policy towards population growth
1- Raise, 2- Maintain, 3- Lower, 4- No intervention

Government policy towards fertility
1- Raise, 2- Maintain, 3- Lower, 4- No intervention

Policy on contraceptive use
1- Major limits (ML), 2- No ML: no support, 3- No ML: indirect support, 4- No ML: direct support

Government policy on internal migration
1- Accelerate trend, 2- Decelerate trend, 3- Reverse trend.
4- No intervention, 5- Maintain trend

Notes

* - Data not yet available for recently unified countries

** - Most recent data

na- Data not available

	Population (thousands) 1990	Growth Rate (percent) 1990-95	Urban Population (percent) 1990-95	Doubling Time (years)	Population (thousands) 2020	Total Fertility Rate 1990-95	Contraceptive Prevalence Rate **	Government Agency for Pop. Policy 1988	Policy on Population Growth 1988	Policy Towards Fertility 1988	Policy on Contraceptive Use 1988	Policy on Internal Migration 1988
Oman	1502	3.75	11	19	4202	7.07	na	2	1	2	2	2
Qatar	368	3.41	89	21	781	5.33	na	2	1	2	2	3
Saudi Arabia	14134	3.84	77	18	39650	7.07	na	2	1	2	1	1
Syrian Arab Republic	12530	3.60	50	19	30924	6.25	19.8	2	4	4	4	2
Turkey	55868	1.95	61	36	83744	3.28	51.0	1	3	3	4	2
United Arab Emirates	1589	2.24	78	31	2559	4.31	na	2	4	4	2	1
Yemen*	9196	3.70	25	19	24953	7.58	50.0	1	4	3	4	4
OCEANIA												
Australia	16873	1.18	85	59	22309	1.80	na	2	4	4	2	4
Fiji	764	1.51	39	47	1083	2.78	41.0	1	4	3	4	3
Kiribati	66	0.99	na	71	80	na	na	1	3	3	4	3
Nauru	9	1.39	na	50	12	na	na	2	1	2	4	4
New Zealand	3392	0.82	84	85	4051	1.95	69.5	2	4	4	3	4
Papua New Guinea	3874	2.28	16	31	6828	4.84	na	2	3	4	4	4
Samoa	168	0.33	na	212	172	na	na	2	3	3	4	4
Solomon Islands	320	3.10	na	23	680	na	na	1	4	4	4	4
Tonga	95	-0.23	na	-	89	na	na	2	3	3	4	2
Tuvalu	9	1.72	na	41	12	na	na	2	3	3	4	2
Vanuatu	158	2.80	na	25	307	na	na	2	4	4	4	4
EUROPE	**498371**	**0.23**	**73**	**299**	**516401**	**1.72**	**na**					
WESTERN EUROPE	**156878**	**0.17**	**81**	**412**	**157563**	**1.61**	**na**					
Austria	7583	0.05	58	1458	7441	1.50	71.4	2	4	4	3	2
Belgium	9845	0.00	97	70000	9501	1.65	81.0	2	4	4	3	4
France	56138	0.35	74	198	60169	1.82	78.7	1	1	1	3	3
Germany, Federal Republic of *	61324	-0.07	87	-	56499	1.43	77.9	1	4	4	3	2
Liechtenstein	28	0.00	na	-	28	na	na	2	1	1	2	4
Luxembourg	373	0.18	84	393	366	1.52	na	2	2	1	2	4
Monaco	28	0.70	na	100	30	na	na	2	1	1	4	4
Netherlands	14951	0.60	89	116	16718	1.60	72.0	1	3	4	4	2
Switzerland	6609	0.22	60	320	6810	1.55	71.2	2	4	4	2	5

Region / Country	Pop (1990)	Growth	% Urban		Pop (2025)	TFR	% Contracept.	Govt agency	Fertility	Contracept.	Growth	Migration
SOUTHERN EUROPE	**144087**	**0.26**	**66**	**269**	**148533**	**1.62**	**na**					
Albania	3245	1.63	35	43	4792	2.70	na	1	2	2	2	3
Greece	10047	0.15	62	458	10139	1.65	na	2	1	1	3	2
Holy See	1	0.00	na	-	1	na	na		4	4	4	4
Italy	57061	0.02	69	3684	54138	1.40	78.0	1	4	1	4	2
Malta	353	0.40	87	173	388	1.85	na	2	4	2	4	4
Portugal	10285	0.28	34	251	10917	1.70	66.3	1	4	4	4	3
San Marino	23	0.85	na	82	25	na	na		4	2	4	4
Spain	39187	0.37	78	190	42122	1.65	59.4	2	2	2	4	4
Yugoslavia	23807	0.48	56	145	25922	1.87	55.0	2	2	2	4	2
NORTHERN EUROPE	**84233**	**0.24**	**84**	**292**	**88144**	**1.82**	**na**					
Denmark	5143	0.06	87	1228	4973	1.50	63.0	2	4	4	4	4
Finland	4975	0.22	60	315	5147	1.65	80.0	2	4	4	4	4
Iceland	253	0.83	91	84	305	1.90	na	2	4	4	4	3
Ireland	3720	0.95	57	74	4808	2.35	na	2	2	2	2	2
Norway	4212	0.28	75	251	4482	1.69	71.0	2	4	4	2	3
Sweden	8444	0.15	84	458	8604	1.87	78.1	2	4	4	4	2
United Kingdom	57237	0.22	89	321	59544	1.83	83.0	1	4	4	4	4
EASTERN EUROPE	**113174**	**0.29**	**65**	**241**	**122161**	**1.94**	**na**					
Bulgaria	9010	0.06	68	1207	8985	1.80	76.0	1	1	1	4	3
Czechoslovakia	15667	0.26	77	267	17061	1.95	95.0	1	2	2	4	5
German Democratic Republic*	16249	-0.04	77	-	15970	1.65	na	1	1	1	4	2
Hungary	10552	-0.08	61	-	10291	1.75	73.1	1	1	1	4	4
Poland	38423	0.49	62	144	44333	2.10	75.0	1	4	4	4	2
Romania	23272	0.46	53	151	25521	2.00	58.0	1	1	1	1	2
USSR												
Byelorussian SSR	na	na	na	-	na	na	na	1	2	2	2	3
Ukrainian S.S.R.	na	na	na	-	na	na	na	1	2	2	2	3
Union of Soviet Socialist Republics	288595	0.68	66	102	343871	2.30	na	1	2	2	2	3
NORTHERN AMERICA	**275865**	**0.71**	**75**	**91**	**326387**	**1.83**	**na**					
Canada	26521	0.77	77	91	31491	1.65	73.1	2	4	4	4	4
United States of America	249224	0.71	75	99	294750	1.85	68.0	2	4	4	4	4

KEY

Government agency for population policy
1- Yes, 2- No, 9- Missing data
Government policy towards population growth
1- Raise, 2- Maintain, 3- Lower, 4- No intervention

Government policy towards fertility
1- Raise, 2- Maintain, 3- Lower, 4- No intervention
Policy on contraceptive use
1- Major limits (ML), 2- No ML: no support,

3- No ML: indirect support, 4- No ML: direct support
Government policy on internal migration
1- Accelerate trend, 2- Decelerate trend, 3- Reverse trend,
4- No intervention, 5- Maintain trend

Sources: Global Population Policy Data Base,
(United Nations, New York, 1990)
World Population Prospects 1990
(United Nations, New York 1991)
Levels and Trends of Contraceptive Use As Assessed in 1988
(United Nations, New York, 1989)

REFERENCES AND NOTES

1. N. Sadik, *The State of World Population 1990* (United Nations Population Fund, New York, 1990).
2. World Commission on Environment and Development, *Our Common Future* (Oxford University Press, Oxford, UK, 1987).
3. United Nations Department of International Economic and Social Affairs, *Population, Resources, Environment and Development* (United Nations, New York, 1984).
4. N. Myers, "The Environmental Dimension to Security Issues", *The Environmentalist*, Vol. 6, pp. 251-257, see also, A. Westing, ed., *Global Resources and International Conflict: Environmental Factors in Strategic Policy and Action* (Oxford University Press, Oxford, UK, 1986).
5. L. Brown, *et al.*, *State of the World 1990* (W. W. Norton, New York, 1990).
6. E. von Weiszacher, *Ord Politik* (Institute for European Environmental Policy, Bonn, Germany, 1990).
7. R. Repetto, *et al.*, *Wasting Assets: Natural Resources in the National Income Accounts* (World Resources Institute, Washington DC, June, 1989).
8. United Nations Population Fund, *Meeting the Population Challenge* (United Nations Population Fund, New York, 1989).
9. F. H. Sanderson, ed., *Agricultural Protections in the Industrial World* (Johns Hopkins University, Baltimore MD, 1990).
10. P. Winglee, "Agricultural Trade Policies of Industrial Countries", *Finance and Development*, Vol. 26, No. 1, 1989, pp. 9-12.
11. J. Zietz and A. Valdes, *Costs of Protectionism to Developing Countries* (The World Bank, Washington DC, 1986).
12. R. P. Shaw, "Rapid Population Growth and Environmental Degradation: Ultimate versus Proximate Factors", *Environmental Conservation*, Vol. 16, 1989, pp. 199-208.
13. United Nations Department of International Economic and Social Affairs, *Consequences of Rapid Population Growth in Developing Countries* (Population Division, Department of International Economic and Social Affairs, United Nations, New York, 1989).
14. United Nations Department of International Economic and Social Affairs, *Global Outlook 2000* (Department of International Economic and Social Affairs, United Nations, New York, 1990).
15. N. Sadik, *Safeguarding the Future* (United Nations Population Fund, New York, 1989).
16. United Nations Department of International Economic and Social Affairs, *World Population Prospects 1990* (United Nations Department of International Economic and Social Affairs, New York, 1991).
17. N. Keyfitz, "The Growing Human Population", *Scientific American*, Vol. 261, 1989, pp. 119-126.
18. T. W. Merrick, "World Population in Transition", *Population Bulletin*, No. 41 (Population Reference Bureau, Washington DC, 1989).
19. P. Demeny, "A Perspective on Long-Term Population Growth", *Population and Development Review*, Vol. 10, 1984, pp. 103-126.
20. N. Keyfitz, "The Limits of Population Forecasting", *Population and Development Review*, Vol. 7, 1981, pp. 579-593.
21. R. Lee, *Long-Run Global Population Forecasts: Critical Appraisal* (Department of Demography and Economics, University of California, Berkeley CA, 1989).
22. World Bank, *World Development Report 1990* (World Bank, Washington DC, 1990).
23. P. R. Ehrlich and A. H. Ehrlich, *The Population Explosion* (Simon and Schuster, New York, 1990).
24. K. Davis, M. S. Berstam and H. M. Sellers, *Population and Resources in a Changing World* (Morrison Institute for Population and Resource Studies, Stanford University, Stanford CA, 1989).

25. D. Pimentel and M. Pimentel, "Land, Energy and Water: the Constraints Governing Ideal U.S. Population Size", *The NPG Forum* (Negative Population Growth, Teaneck NJ, 1989).

26. M. Lipton, *The Poor and the Poorest: Some Interim Findings* (The World Bank, Washington DC, 1985).

27. N. Keyfitz, *Population Growth can Prevent the Development that Would Slow Population Growth* (Population Programme, International Institute for Applied Systems Analysis, Laxenburg, Austria, 1990); see also a version of this paper published in J. Mathews, ed, *Preserving the Global Environment: The Challenge of Shared Leadership* (Norton, New York, 1991), pp. 39-77.

28. N. Myers, "Environmental Degradation and Some Economic Consequences in the Philippines", *Environmental Conservation*, Vol. 15, 1988, pp. 205-214.

29. Food and Agriculture Organization of the United Nations, *Potential Population Supporting Capacities of Lands in the Developing World* (FAO, Rome, 1984). For a popular summary of this report see also: P. Harrison, *Land, Food and People* (FAO, Rome, 1984).

30. Intergovernmental Panel on Climate Change, *Climate Change: The IPCC Scientific Assessment* (Cambridge University Press, Cambridge, UK, 1990).

31. M. Oppenheimer and R. H. Boyle, *Dead Heat: The Race Against the Greenhouse Effect* (Basic Books, New York, 1990).

32. J. Leggett, *Global Warming: The Greenpeace Report* (Oxford University Press, Oxford, UK, 1990).

33. S. H. Schneider, *Global Warming* (Sierra Club Books, San Francisco CA, 1989).

34. Some experts consider these figures to be outdated, since they may have taken inadequate account of carbon dioxide releases from tropical deforestation. Nevertheless, they are retained here for purposes of the present calculation. See P. Harrison, "Too Much Life on Earth?", *New Scientist*, Vol. 126, 1990, pp. 28-29.

35. J. P. Holdren, "Energy in Transition", *Scientific American*, Vol. 263, No. 3, 1990, pp. 109-115.

36. J. M. Dave, *Policy Options for Development in Response to Global Atmospheric Changes: Case Study for India for Greenhouse Effect Causes* (Nehru University, New Delhi, India, 1988).

37. US Office of Technology Assessment, *International Policy Dimensions of Global Warming: U.S. Influence and Regional Trends* (US Office of Technology Assessment, Washington DC, 1990).

38. G. C. Daily and P. R. Ehrlich, *An Exploratory Model of the Impact of Rapid Climate Change on the World Food Situation* (The Morrison Institute for Population and Resource Studies, Stanford University, Stanford CA, 1990).

39. M. Parry, *Climate Change and World Agriculture* (Earthscan Publications Ltd., London, UK, 1990).

40. D. Pimentel, *et al.*, *Offsetting Potential Global Climate Changes on Food Production* (College of Agriculture, Cornell University, Ithaca NY, 1990).

41. B. Smit and L. Ludlow, "Implications of a Global Climatic Warming for Agriculture: A Review and Appraisal", *Journal of Environmental Quality*, Vol. 17, 1988, pp. 519-527.

42. D. Wiks, "Estimating the Consequences of Carbon Dioxide-Induced Climate Change on North American Grain Agriculture Using General Circulation Model Information", *Climate Change*, Vol. 13, 1988, pp. 19-42.

43. E. Arrhenius and T. Waltz, *The Greenhouse Effect: Implications for Economic Development* (The World Bank, Washington DC, 1990).

44. Delft Hydraulics, *Criteria for Assessing Vulnerability to Sea Level Rise: A Global Inventory of High Risk Areas*, (United Nations Environment Programme, Nairobi, Kenya, 1989).

45. P. Vellinga and S. P. Leatherman, "Sea Level Rise: Consequences and Policies", *Climatic Change*, Vol. 15, 1989, pp. 175-189.

46. D. Hinrichsen, *Our Common Seas: Coasts in Crisis* (Earthscan Publications Ltd., London, UK, 1990).

47. J. E. Bardach, "Global Warming and the Coastal Zone: Some Effects on Sites and

Activities", in *Proceedings of the Conference on Developing Policies for Responding to Future Climatic Changes* (Villach, Austria, 20 September-2 October, 1987).

48. J. D. Milliman, J. M. Broadus and F. Gable, "Environment and Economic Implications of Rising Sea Level and Subsiding Deltas: The Nile and Bengal Examples", *Ambio*, Vol. 18, 1989, pp. 340-345.

49. R. E. Benedick, *Ozone Diplomacy: New Directions in Safeguarding the Planet* (The Conservation Foundation, Washington DC, 1990).

50. R. Jones and T. Wigley, eds., *Ozone Depletion: Health and Environmental Consequences* (Wiley, Sussex, UK, 1990).

51. I. Mintzer, W. R. Moomaw and A. S. Miller, *Protecting the Ozone Shield: Strategies for Phasing Out CFCs During the 1990s* (World Resources Institute, Washington DC, 1990).

52. S. L. Roan, *Ozone Crisis: The 15-Year Evolution of a Sudden Global Emergency* (Wiley, New York, 1989).

53. A. Chisholm and R. Dumsday, eds., *Land Degradation: Policies and Problems* (Cambridge University Press, New York, 1987).

54. M. K. Tolba, "Our Biological Heritage Under Siege", *BioScience*, Vol. 39, 1989, pp. 725-728.

55. J. R. Anderson and J. Thampapillai, *Soil Conservation in Developing Countries: Project and Policy Interventions* (The World Bank, Washington DC, 1990).

56. J. Boardman, J. A. Dearing and I. D. L. Foster, eds., *Soil Erosion on Agricultural Land* (Wiley, New York, 1990).

57. R. Lal, "Effects of Soil Erosion on Crop Productivity", *CRC Critical Reviews in Plant Science*, Vol. 5, 1987, pp. 303-367.

58. D. Pimentel, ed., *World Soil Erosion and Conservation* (Cambridge University Press, Cambridge, UK, 1991).

59. D. Pimentel, *et al.*, "World Food Economy and the Soil Erosion Crisis", *Environmental Biology Report*, Vol. 86, 1985.

60. A. Sfeir-Younis, *Soil Conservation in Developing Countries – A Background Report* (The World Bank, Washington DC, 1986).

61. R. Repetto, "Soil Loss and Population Pressure on Java", *Ambio*, Vol. 15, 1986, pp. 14-18.

62. E. B. Barbier, "The Farm-Level Economics of Soil Conservation: The Uplands of Java", *Land Economics*, Vol. 66, 1990, pp. 201-211.

63. A. T. Birowo and D. Prabowo, "The Pressure on Natural Resources in Indonesian Agricultural Development", in *Agriculture in a Turbulent World Economy* (Institute of Agricultural Economics, Oxford, UK, 1986).

64. W. B. Magrath and P. Arens, *The Costs of Soil Erosion on Java – A Natural Resource Accounting Approach* (World Resources Institute, Washington DC, 1987).

65. J. A. Dixon, D. E. James and P. B. Sherman, *The Economics of Dryland Management* (Earthscan Publications Ltd., London, UK, 1990).

66. H. E. Dregne and C. J. Tucker, "Desert Encroachment", *Desertification Control Bulletin*, Vol. 16, 1988, pp. 16-19.

67. G. P. Hekstra and D. M. Liverman, "Global Food Futures and Desertification", *Climatic Change*, Vol. 9, 1986, pp. 59-66.

68. J. A. Mabbutt, "A New Global Assessment of the Status and Trends of Desertification", *Environmental Conservation*, Vol. 11, 1984, pp. 103-113.

69. R. Nelson, *Dryland Management, the "Desertification" Problem* (The World Bank, Washington DC, 1990).

70. P. L. Blaikie, *Political Economy of Soil Erosion in Developing Countries* (Longman, London, UK, 1985).

71. R. V. Garcia, *Nature Pleads Not Guilty* (Pergamon Press, Oxford, UK, 1981).

72. R. W. Franke and B. H. Chasin, *Seeds of Famine: Ecological Destruction and the Development Dilemma in the West African Sahel* (Universe Books, revised edition, New York, 1984).

73. A. G. Hill, *Demographic Responses to Food Shortages in the Sahel* (Food and Agriculture Organization of the United Nations, Rome, 1987).

74. A. Grainger, *The Threatening Desert* (Earthscan Publications Ltd., London, UK, 1990).
75. J. A. Mabbutt, "Impacts of Carbon Dioxide Warming on Climate and Man in the Semi-Arid Tropics", *Climatic Change*, Vol. 15, 1989, pp. 191-221.
76. R. Repetto, *Population, Resources, Environment: An Uncertain Future* (Population Reference Bureau, Washington DC, 1987).
77. L. A. Paulino, *Food in the Third World: Past Trends and Projections to 2000* (International Food Policy Research Institute, Washington DC, 1986).
78. L. R. Brown, *The Changing World Food Prospect: The Nineties and Beyond* (Worldwatch Institute, Washington DC, 1989).
79. D. Hinrichsen, "Nepal: Struggling for a Common Future", *Populi*, Vol. 18, 1991, pp. 43-51.
80. W. G. V. Balchin, "Water – A World Problem", *International Journal of Environmental Studies*, Vol. 25, 1985, pp. 141-148.
81. M. Falkenmark, *The Massive Water Penury Now Threatening Africa – Why Isn't it Addressed?* (Stockholm Group for Studies on Natural Resource Management, Stockholm, Sweden, 1988); see also a published version of this paper in *Ambio*, Vol. 18, 1989, pp. 112-118.
82. M. Falkenmark and T. Chapman, eds., *Comparative Hydrology: An Ecological Approach to Land and Water Resources* (UNESCO, Paris, France, 1989).
83. M. Falkenmark, "Water Scarcity and Food Production in Africa", in D. Pimentel and C. W. Hall, eds., *Food and Natural Resources* (Academic Press, New York, 1989), pp. 163-189.
84. J. W. M. la Riviere, "Threats to the World's Water", *Scientific American*, Vol. 261, 1989, pp. 48-55.
85. S. Postel, *Water for Agriculture: Facing the Limits* (Worldwatch Institute, Washington DC, 1989).
86. R. Repetto, *Skimming the Water: Rent-Seeking and the Performance of Public Irrigation Systems* (World Resources Institute, Washington DC, 1986).
87. H. Shuval, A. Adin, B. Fattal, E. Rawits and P. Yekutiel, *Integrated Resource Recovery, Water Irrigation in Developing Countries, Health Effects and Technical Solutions* (The World Bank, Technical Paper No. 51, Washington DC, 1986).
88. United Nations, *Water Resources: Progress in the Implementation of the Mar de Plata Action Plan* (United Nations Economic and Social Council, New York, 1987).
89. M. Falkenmark, "Global Water Issues Confronting Humanity", *Journal of Peace Research*, Vol. 27, 1990, pp. 177-190.
90. UNICEF, *The State of the World's Children* (UNICEF, New York, 1985).
91. S. M. Nor and H. T. Tang, *Forest Conservation in Malaysia: A Reappraisal* (Forest Research Institute, Kepong, Kuala Lumpur, Malaysia, 1980).
92. M. Falkenmark, "Fresh Water – Time for a Modified Approach", *Ambio*, Vol. 15, 1986, pp. 192-200.
93. L. R. Brown *et al.*, *State of the World 1989* (W. W. Norton, New York, 1989).
94. N. D. Jayal, *Destruction of Water Resources – The Most Critical Ecological Crisis of East Asia* (Paper presented at the 16th Technical Meeting of IUCN, Madrid, Spain, 5-14 November, 1984).
95. W. R. Gasser, *Survey of Irrigation in Eight Asian Nations* (Foreign Agricultural Economic Report No. 165, Economics and Statistics Service, US Dept of Agriculture, Washington DC, 1981).
96. J. C. Cool, *Factors Affecting Pressure on Mountain Resource Systems* (Agriculture Development Council, Kathmandu, Nepal, 1984).
97. H. J. Leonard, *Natural Resources and Economic Development in Central America* (Transaction Books, New Brunswick NJ, 1987).
98. M. Falkenmark, "Water-Related Constraints to African Development in the Next Few Decades", in *Water for the Future: Hydrology in Perspective* (IAHS Publication, No. 164, 1987).
99. M. Falkenmark, "New Ecological Approach to the Water Cycle: Ticket to the Future", *Ambio*, Vol. 13, 1984, pp. 152-160.

POPULATION, RESOURCES AND THE ENVIRONMENT

100. C. Widstrand, *Water and Society II: Water Conflicts and Research Priorities* (Pergamon Press, New York, 1980).
101. P. Jabber, "Egypt's Crisis: America's Dilemma", *Foreign Affairs,* Vol. 64, 1986, pp. 960-980.
102. World Bank, *World Development Report 1986* (The World Bank, Washington DC, 1986).
103. M. A. Kishk, "Land Degradation in the Nile Valley", *Ambio*, Vol. 15, 1986, pp. 226-230.
104. E. D. Stains, *Irrigation Briefing Paper* (Office of Irrigation and Land Development, US AID, Cairo, Egypt, 1987).
105. R. S. Bradley, H. F. Diaz, J. K. Eishcard, P. D. Jones, P. M. Kelly and C. M. Goodess, "Precipitation Fluctuations over the Northern Hemisphere Land Areas Since the Mid-19th century", *Science*, Vol. 237, 1987, pp. 171-175.
106. D. Jovanovic, "Ethiopia's Interests in the Division of the Nile River Waters", *Water International*, Vol. 10, 1985, pp. 82-85.
107. J. R. Starr, and D. C. Stoll, *U.S. Foreign Policy on Water Resources in the Middle East* (Center for Strategic and International Studies, Washington DC, 1988).
108. J. Waterbury, "Legal and Institutional Arrangements for Managing Water Resources in the Nile Basin", *Water Resources Development*, Vol. 3, 1987, pp. 92-103.
109. D. Whittington and K. E. Haynes, "Nile Water for Whom? Emerging Conflicts in Water Allocation for Agricultural Expansion in Egypt and Sudan", in P. Beaumont and K. McLaughlin, eds., *Agricultural Development in the Middle East* (Wiley, New York, 1985).
110. A. A. Cashed, "The Nile – One River and Nine Countries", *Journal of Hydrology*, Vol. 53, 1981, pp. 53-84.
111. M. Shahin, *Hydrology of the Nile Basin* (Elsevier Publishers, New York, 1985).
112. J. K. Cooley, "The War Over Water", *Foreign Policy*, Vol. 54, 1984, pp. 3-26.
113. R. C. Matson and T. Naff, *Water in the Middle East: Conflict or Cooperation* (Westview Press, Boulder CO, 1984).
114. H. I. Shuval, "The Development of Water Re-Use in Israel", *Ambio*, Vol. 16, 1987, pp. 186-190.
115. N. Myers, *Deforestation Rates in Tropical Forests and Their Climatic Implications* (Friends of the Earth, London, UK, 1989).
116. M. Palo and J. Salmi, eds., *Deforestation or Development in the Third World* (Finnish Forest Research Institute, Helsinki, 1988).
117. W. J. Peters and L. F. Neuenschwander, *Slash and Burn Farming in Third World Forests* (University of Idaho Press, Moscow ID, 1988).
118. A. Grainger, *TROPFORM: A Model of Future Tropical Hardwood Supplies* (Resources for the Future, Washington DC, 1987).
119. D. Southgate and C. F. Runge, *The Institutional Origins of Deforestation in Latin America* (Department of Agricultural and Applied Economics, University of Minnesota, Minneapolis MN, 1990).
120. J.-P. Malingreau and C. J. Tucker, "Large-Scale Deforestation in the Southern Amazon Basin of Brazil", *Ambio*, Vol. 17, 1988, pp. 49-55.
121. R. Sinha, *Landlessness: A Growing Problem* (Food and Agriculture Organization of the United Nations, Rome, 1984).
122. D. Anderson and R. Fishwick, *Fuelwood Consumption and Deforestation in African Countries* (The World Bank, Washington DC, 1984).
123. Food and Agriculture Organization of the United Nations, *An Interim Report on the State of Forest Resources in the Developing Countries* (FAO, Rome, 1987).
124. B. Munslow *et al.*, *The Fuelwood Trap* (Earthscan Publications Ltd., London, UK, 1988).
125. H. M. Peskin, *Accounting for Natural Resource Depletion and Degradation in Developing Countries* (Environment Department Working Paper No. 13, The World Bank, Washington DC, 1989).
126. S. Postel and L. Heise, *Reforesting the Earth* (Worldwatch Institute, Washington DC,

1988).

127. C. P. Shea, *Renewable Energy: Today's Contribution, Tomorrow's Promise* (Worldwatch Institute, Washington DC, 1988).

128. T. S. Wood and S. Baldwin, "Fuelwood and Charcoal Use in Developing Countries", *Annual Review of Energy*, Vol. 10, 1985, pp. 407-429.

129. S. K. Kumar and D. Hochkiss, *Consequences of Deforestation for Women's Time Allocation, Agricultural Production and Nutrition in Hill Areas of Nepal* (International Food Policy Research Institute, Washington DC, 1988).

130. H. M. Peskin, *National Accounts and the Development Process: Illustration with Tanzania* (Resources for the Future, Washington DC, 1984).

131. K. Newcombe, *An Economic Justification for Rural Afforestation: The Case of Ethiopia* (The World Bank, Washington DC, 1984).

132. D. W. Pearce, *The Economics of Natural Resource Management: Issues Paper* (The World Bank, Washington DC, 1986).

133. T. L. Erwin, "The Tropical Forest Canopy: The Heart of Biotic Diversity", in E. O. Wilson, ed., *Biodiversity* (National Academy Press, Washington DC, 1988), pp. 123-129.

134. N. Myers, "Threatened Biotas: "Hot Spots" in Tropical Forests", *The Environmentalist*, Vol. 8, 1988, pp. 187-208.

135. N. Myers, "The Biodiversity Challenge: Expanded Hot Spot Analysis", *The Environmentalist*, Vol. 10, 1990, pp. 243-256.

136. P. H. Raven, *We're Killing Our World: The Global Ecosystem in Crisis* (MacArthur Foundation Occasional Paper, The MacArthur Foundation, Chicago, Illinois, 1987).

137. M. E. Soule, ed., *Conservation Biology: The Science of Scarcity and Diversity* (Sinauer Associates, Sunderland MA, 1986).

138. E. O. Wilson, "Threats to Biodiversity", *Scientific American*, Vol. 261, 1989, pp. 108-116.

139. N. Myers, *A Wealth of Wild Species: Storehouse for Human Welfare* (Westview Press, Boulder CO, 1983); and G. Lean, D. Hinrichsen and A. Markham, *WWF Atlas of the Environment* (Prentice Hall Press, New York, 1990), pp. 127-132.

140. United Nations Development Programme, *Human Development Report 1990* (Oxford University Press, Oxford, UK, 1990).

141. L. Timberlake and L. Thomas, *When the Bough Breaks* (Earthscan Publications Ltd., London, UK, 1990).

142. UNICEF, *State of the World's Children* (UNICEF, New York, 1990).

143. B. A. Carlson and T. M. Wardlaw, *A Global, Regional and Country Assessment of Child Malnutrition* (UNICEF, New York, 1990).

144. United Nations Environment Programme and United Nations Children's Fund, *Children and the Environment* (UNEP, Nairobi, Kenya, and UNCF, New York, 1990).

145. K. R. Smith, *Biofuels, Air Pollution, and Health: A Global Review* (Plenum Press, New York, 1987).

146. B. Herz and A. R. Measham, *The Safe Motherhood Initiative: Proposals for Action* (The World Bank, Washington DC, 1987).

147. E. Royston and S. Armstrong, eds., *Preventing Maternal Deaths* (World Health Organization, Geneva, 1989).

148. N. Yinger, "Focus on Maternal Mortality", *Population Today*, Vol. 18, 1990, pp. 6-7.

149. J. L. Jacobson, *The Global Politics of Abortion* (Worldwatch Institute, Washington DC, 1990).

150. P. Smyke, *Women and Health* (Zed Books, London, UK, 1991).

151. I. Dankelman and J. Davidson, *Women and Environment in the Third World: Alliance for the Future* (Earthscan Publications Ltd., London, 1988).

152. M. Ladjali and P. Huston, "Listen to Women First", *People*, Vol. 17, 1990, pp. 21-22.

153. M. C. J. Cruz and I. Zosa-Feranil, *Policy Implications of Population Pressure in the Philippine Uplands* (Dept of Environmental Studies, University of the Philippines, Los Banos, and the Population Institute, University of the Philippines, Diliman, Philippines, 1987).

154. N. Myers, "The World's Forests and Human Populations: The Environmental

Interconnections", *Population and Development Review*, Vol. 16, 1991, pp. 1-15.

155. D. A. Schumann and W. L. Partridge, eds., *The Human Ecology of Tropical Land Settlement in Latin America* (Westview Press, Boulder CO, 1989).

156. D. E. Bloom and R. B. Freeman, "The Effects of Rapid Population Growth on Labor Supply and Employment in Developing Countries", *Population and Development Review*, Vol. 12, 1986, pp. 381-414.

157. R. Marshall, "Jobs: The Shifting Structure of Global Employment" in J. W. Sewell and S. K. Tucker, eds., *Growth, Exports and Jobs in a Changing World Economy* (Transaction Books, New Brunswick NJ, 1988), pp. 167-193.

158. L. Bilderback, "Migration", *Bulletin of the Atomic Scientists*, Vol. 42, 1986, pp. 33-37.

159. World Bank, *Sub-Saharan Africa: From Crisis to Sustainable Growth* (The World Bank, Washington DC, 1989).

160. B. Dasgupta, *The Rural Landless: A Synthesis of Country Case Studies* (Food and Agriculture Organization of the United Nations, Rome, 1985).

161. Food and Agriculture Organization of the United Nations, *African Agriculture, the Next 25 Years: The Land Resource Base* (FAO, Rome, 1986).

162. S. Ahmed, *Landlessness in Rural Asia: An Overview* (Center for Integrated Rural Development for Asia and the Pacific, Dhaka, Bangladesh, 1987).

163. S. Fernando, *National Assessment of Rural Landlessness, Sri Lanka* (Food and Agriculture Organization of the United Nations, Bangkok, 1985).

164. J. Hartmann, *Landlessness and Rural Employment in Indonesia* (Food and Agriculture Organization of the United Nations, Bangkok, 1985).

165. G. D. Ness and H. Ando, *The Land is Shrinking: Population Planning in Asia* (Johns Hopkins University Press, Baltimore MD, 1984).

166. S. Tongpan, *Landlessness in Thailand* (Food and Agriculture Organization of the United Nations, Bangkok, 1985).

167. P. O. Alila, G. Wanjohi and K. Kinyanjui, *The Rural Landlessness Situation in Kenya* (Food and Agriculture Organization of the United Nations, Rome, 1985).

168. H. Caycho, *Campesinos sin Tieras en Peru* (Food and Agriculture Organization of the United Nations, Rome, 1985).

169. B. P. Rangel, *Evaluacion Nacional de la Situacion de los Campesinos sin Tieras en Mexico* (Food and Agriculture Organization of the United Nations, Rome, 1985).

170. H. Tollini and A. Veiga, *El Campesino sin Tieras en Brazil* (Food and Agriculture Organization of the United Nations, Rome, 1985).

171. L. R. Brown and J. L. Jacobson, *The Future of Urbanization: Facing the Ecological and Economic Constraints* (Worldwatch Institute, Washington DC, 1987).

172. J. Hardoy and D. Satterthwaite, *Squatter Citizen: Life in the Urban Third World* (Earthscan Publications Ltd., London, UK, 1989).

173. J. Hardoy and D. Satterthwaite, *Environmental Problems in Third World Cities: A Global Problem Ignored?* (International Institute for Environment and Development, London, UK, 1990).

174. J. T. Martin, I. Ness, and S. T. Collins, *Book of World City Rankings* (The Free Press, London, UK, 1986).

175. United Nations, *The Prospects of World Urbanization: Revised as of 1984-85* (United Nations, Population Division, New York, 1987).

176. D. Drakakis-Smith, *The Third World City* (Methuen, New York, 1987).

177. United Nations, *The Prospects of World Urbanization* (United Nations, Population Division, New York, 1988).

178. R. S. McNamara, "The Population Problem: Time Bomb or Myth", *Foreign Affairs*, Vol. 62, 1984, pp. 1107-1131.

179. T. Panayotou, *The Economics of Environmental Degradation: Problems, Causes and Responses* (Harvard Institute for International Development, Cambridge MA, 1990).

180. H. F. French, "You Are What You Breathe", *World Watch*, Vol. 3, 1990, pp. 27-34.

181. A. Agarwal and S. Narain, *Towards Green Villages* (Centre for Science and Environment, New Delhi, India, 1989).

182. R. E. Bilsborrow and P. DeLargy, *Population Growth, Natural Resource Use and*

Migration in the Third World: The Cases of Guatemala and Sudan (Carolina Population Center, University of North Carolina, Chapel Hill NC, 1990).

183. B. Bowonder, S. S. R. Prasad and N. V. M. Unni, "Deforestation Around Urban Centers in India", *Environmental Conservation*, Vol. 14, 1987, pp. 23-28.

184. J. L. Jacobson, *Environmental Refugees: A Yardstick of Habitability* (Worldwatch Institute, Washington DC, 1988).

185. N. Myers, *Environment and Security* (W. W. Norton, New York, 1991, in press).

186. E. El Hinnawi, *Environmental Refugees* (United Nations Environment Programme, Nairobi, Kenya, 1985).

187. B. Commoner, "Rapid Population Growth and Environmental Stress" in *Consequences of Rapid Population Growth in Developing Countries* (Proceedings of the United Nations Expert Group Meeting, 23-26 August, 1988, United Nations, New York).

188. B. Commoner, *Making Peace with the Planet* (Pantheon Books, New York, 1990).

189. G. Rodgers, *Poverty and Population: Approaches and Evidence* (International Labour Office, Geneva, Switzerland, 1984).

190. S. Camp and J. Speidel, *The International Human Suffering Index* (Population Crisis Committee, Washington DC, 1987).

191. R. S. Chen, W. H. Bender, R. W. Kates, E. Messer and S. R. Millman, *The Hunger Report* (World Hunger Program, Brown University, Providence RI, 1990).

192. A. B. Durning, *Action at the Grassroots: Fighting Poverty and Environmental Decline* (Worldwatch Institute, Washington DC, 1989).

193. Food and Agriculture Organization of the United Nations, *The State of Food and Agriculture 1990* (FAO, Rome, 1990).

194. N. Alexandrotos, ed., *World Agriculture Toward 2000: An FAO Study* (New York University Press, New York, 1988).

195. M. Berger and M. Buvinic, eds., *The Informal Sector, Microenterprise and Women's Work in Latin America* (Kumarin Press, Hartford CT, 1990).

196. J. Leslie and M. Paolisso, eds., *Women's Work and Child Welfare in the Third World* (Westview Press, Boulder CO, 1989). See also: J. Leslie, *Women's Time: A Factor in the Use of Child Survival Technologies?* (International Center for Research on Women, Washington DC, 1988).

197. M. Lycette, *Improving Women's Access to Credit in the Third World: Policy and Project Recommendations* (International Center for Research on Women, Washington DC, 1984).

198. H. Pietila and J. Vickers, *Making Women Matter: The Role of the United Nations* (Zed Books, London, UK, 1990).

199. N. Sadik, *Investing in Women: The Focus of the 1990s* (United Nations Population Fund, New York, 1989).

200. J. Vickers, *Women and the World Economic Crisis* (Zed Books, London, UK, 1991).

201. A. Rodda, *Women and the Environment* (Zed Books, London, UK, 1991).

202. P. Harrison, "Fragile Future", *Sunday Observer Magazine*, May 5, 1989 (London, UK).

203. J. Davidson, *Women and the Environment* (University College London, London, UK, 1990).

204. P. R. Ehrlich, G. C. Daily, A. H. Ehrlich, P. Matson and P. Vitousek, *Global Change and Carrying Capacity: Implications for Life on Earth* (Stanford Institute for Population and Resource Studies, Stanford University, Stanford CA, 1989).

205. H. E. Daly, and J. B. Cobb Jr., *For the Common Good* (Beacon Press, Boston MA, 1989).

206. D. Mahar, ed. *Rapid Population Growth and Human Carrying Capacity* (World Bank Staff Working Paper No. 690, The World Bank, Washington DC, 1985).

207. J. L. Simon, *Population Matters: People, Resources, Environment and Immigration* (Transaction Publishers, New Brunswick NJ, 1990).

208. US Department of Agriculture, *World Agricultural Production* (Foreign Agricultural Service, US Department of Agriculture, Washington DC, 1990).

209. N. Myers, "Environmental Security: The Case of South Asia", *International*

Environmental Affairs, Vol. 1, 1989, pp. 138-154.
210. World Bank, *World Development Report 1987* (The World Bank, Washington DC, 1987).
211. Government of Pakistan, *Environmental Profile of Pakistan* (Environment and Urban Affairs Division, Government of Pakistan, Islamabad, Pakistan, 1986).
212. National Conservation Strategy Secretariat (of Pakistan), *National Conservation Strategy* (National Conservation Secretariat, Islamabad, Pakistan, 1989).
213. C. P. R. Nottidge, G. Schreiber and A. Q. Sheikh, *Pakistan: Environmental Rehabilitation, Protection and Management* (The World Bank, Islamabad, Pakistan, 1985).
214. World Bank, *Women in Pakistan: An Economic and Social Strategy* (The World Bank, Washington DC, 1990).
215. K. Mumtaz and F. Shaheed, *Women of Pakistan: One Step Forward, Two Steps Back* (Zed Press, London, UK, 1990).
216. A. K. Biswas, "Environmental Concerns in Pakistan, With Special Reference to Water and Forests", *Environmental Conservation*, Vol. 14, 1987, pp. 319-328.
217. N. Amjad and J. Mohammad, *The State of Forestry in Pakistan* (Pakistan Forestry Institute, Peshawar, Islamabad, Pakistan, 1982).
218. W. F. Megahan and A. M. Chima, "Watershed Management in Pakistan – Past, Present and Future", *Journal of Forestry*, Vol. 78, 1980, pp. 217-219.
219. M. I. Sheikh, Personal Communication, May 17, 1987 (Office of the Director General of the Pakistan Forestry Institute, Peshawar, Pakistan).
220. R. Schwass, *National Conservation Strategy for Pakistan: Preliminary Appraisal* (Faculty of Environmental Studies, York University, Toronto, Canada, 1986).
221. World Bank, *Pakistan: Forestry Sector Survey* (The World Bank, Washington DC, 1978).
222. Pakistan Forestry Institute, *Forestry, Watershed, Range and Wildlife Management in Pakistan* (Pakistan Forestry Institute, Peshawar, Pakistan, 1983).
223. Food and Agriculture Organization of the United Nations, *Production Yearbook 1987* (FAO, Rome, 1988).
224. K. Mohtadullah, personal communication, letter of May 19, 1987 (Office of the Director, Pakistan Water and Power Development Authority, Islamabad, Pakistan).
225. S. Ahmad, M. Yasin and G. R. Sandhu, *Efficient Irrigation Management Supplements: Land Drainage* (Pakistan Agricultural Research Council, Islamabad, Pakistan, 1987).
226. S. M. H. Bokhari, "Case Study on Waterlogging and Salinity Problems in Pakistan", *Water Supply and Management*, Vol. 4, 1980, pp. 171-192.
227. B. A. Malik, *Pakistan's Limited Water Resources and Growing Demand* (International Commission on Irrigation and Drainage, Islamabad, Pakistan, 1980).
228. K. Mohtadullah, *Sector Report on Water Development* (National Conservation Strategy Secretariat, Islamabad, Pakistan, 1989).
229. World Bank, *Pakistan Environmental Rehabilitation, Protection and Management: Reconnaissance Mission Report* (The World Bank, Washington DC, 1985).
230. W. Irian, *Sector Report on Population Growth* (National Conservation Strategy, Islamabad, Pakistan, 1989).
231. S. M. Khan, "Management of River and Reservoir Sedimentation in Pakistan", *Water Resources Journal*, Vol. 149, 1986, pp. 40-43.
232. United Nations, *Trends in Population Studies* (United Nations, Document No. ST/ESA/SER.A/114, New York, 1989).
233. United Nations, *Levels and Trends of Contraceptive Use as Assessed in 1988* (United Nations, Document No. ST/SER/SER.A/110, New York, 1989).
234. S. K. Sinha, "The 1982-83 Drought in India: Magnitude and Impact", in M. Glantz, R. Katz and M. Krenz, eds., *The Societal Impacts Associated with the 1982-83 Worldwide Anomalies*, 1987, pp. 37-42.
235. J. C. Noutiyal and P. H. Babor, "Forestry in the Himalayas", *Interdisciplinary Science Reviews*, Vol. 10, pp. 27-41, 1985.
236. J. S. Singh, ed., *Environmental Regeneration in the Himalayas: Concepts and Strategies* (Gyanodaya Prakashan, Nainital, India, 1985).

237. A. Agarwal, R. Chopra and K. Sharma, eds., *The State of India's Environment 1982* (Centre for Science and Environment, New Delhi, India, 1982).
238. B. B. Vohra, *Management of Natural Resources: Urgent Need for Fresh Thinking* (Advisory Board on Energy and Water, Government of India, New Delhi, India, 1986).
239. M. L. Dewan and S. Sharma, *People's Participation as a Key to Himalayan Eco-System Development* (Centre for Policy Research, New Delhi, India, 1985).
240. N. Myers, "Environmental Repercussions of Deforestation in the Himalayas", *Journal of World Forest Resource Management*, Vol. 2, 1986, pp. 63-72.
241. P. Hendry, *Food and Population: Beyond Five Billion*, Population Bulletin, Vol. 43, No. 2 (Population Reference Bureau, Washington DC, 1988).
242. S. L. Bahugna, *Himalayan Trauma: Forests, Faults, Floods* (Gandhi Peace Foundation, New Delhi, India, 1978).
243. A. Agarwal *et al.*, *The Wrath of Nature: The Impact of Environmental Destruction on Floods and Droughts* (Centre for Science and Environment, New Delhi, India, 1987).
244. Indian National Institute of Hydrology, *Forest Influences on Hydrological Parameters: Status Report* (Indian National Institute of Hydrology, Roorkee, India, 1986).
245. High Level Committee on Floods, *Report on the Emergent Crisis* (High Level Committee on Floods, Government of India, New Delhi, India, 1983).
246. V. V. D. Narayana and R. Babu, "Estimate of Soil Erosion in India", *Journal of Irrigation and Drainage Engineering*, Vol. 109, 1983, pp. 419-434.
247. K. Jalees, "Loss of Productive Soil in India", *International Journal of Environmental Studies*, Vol. 24, 1985, pp. 245-250.
248. Ministry of Agriculture, Government of India, *The State of India's Agriculture 1982* (Ministry of Agriculture, New Delhi, India, 1983).
249. D. C. Das, Y. P. Bali and R. N. Kaul, "Soil Conservation in Multiple Purpose River Valley Catchments", *Indian Journal of Soil Conservation*, Vol. 9, 1981, pp. 6-20.
250. Food and Agriculture Organization of the United Nations, *Agriculture: Toward 2000* (FAO, Rome, 1981).
251. F. H. Sanderson, "World Food Prospects to the Year 2000", *Food Policy*, Vol. 9, 1984, pp. 363-373.
252. M. S. Swaminathan and S. K. Sinha, eds., *Global Aspects of Food Production* (Tycooly International Press, Dublin, Ireland, 1986).
253. F. H. Sanderson and S. Roy, *Food Trends and Prospects in India* (The Brookings Institution, Washington DC, 1979).
254. A. Agarwal and S. Narain, *The State of India's Environment 1984-1985: The Second Citizen's Report* (Centre for Science and Environment, New Delhi, India, 1985).
255. D. Seckler and R. K. Sampath, *Production and Poverty in Indian Agriculture* (International School for Agricultural and Resource Development, Colorado State University, Fort Collins CO, 1985).
256. I. Singh, *Small Farmers and the Landless in South Asia* (The World Bank, Washington DC, 1981).
257. P. H. Gleick, *Global Climatic Changes and Geopolitics: Pressures on Developed and Developing Countries* (Paper presented at conference on Climate and Geo-Sciences, Louvain-la-Neuve, Belgium, 22-27 May, 1988; Energy and Resources Group, University of California, Berkeley CA).
258. M. B. Davis, "Climatic Instability, Time Lags and Community Disequilibrium" in J. Daimond and T. J. Case, eds., *Community Ecology* (Harper and Row, New York, 1986), pp. 269-284.
259. K. A. Emanuel, "The Dependence of Hurricane Intensity on Climate", *Nature*, Vol. 326, 1987, pp. 483-485.
260. Zong-Ci Zhao and W. W. Kellogg, "Sensitivity of Soil Moisture to Doubling of Carbon Dioxide in Climate Model Experiments, Part II, The Asian Monsoon Region", *Journal of Climate*, Vol. 1, 1980, pp. 367-378.
261. G. Porter and D. J. Ganapin, *Resources, Population and the Philippines' Future* (World Resources Institute, Washington DC, 1988).
262. World Bank, *Philippines: Environment and Natural Resource Management Study* (The

World Bank, Washington DC, 1989).

263. Agricultural Policy Strategy Team, *Agenda for Action for the Philippine Rural Sector* (Agricultural Policy Research Program, University of the Philippines, Los Banos, Philippines, 1986).

264. D. M. Kummer, *Deforestation in the Post-War Philippines* (Department of Geography, Boston University, Boston MA, 1989).

265. A. V. Revilla, *Policy and Program Agenda for the Forest Resources Management Sub-Sector* (College of Forestry, University of the Philippines, Los Banos, Philippines, 1987).

266. D. J. Ganapin, "Forest Resources and Timber Trade in the Philippines", in *Proceedings of the Conference on Forest Resources Crisis in the Third World*, Kuala Lumpur, 6-8 September, 1986 (Sahabat Alam Malaysia, Kuala Lumpur, Malaysia, 1987).

267. M. C. J. Cruz, I. Zosa-Feranil and C. L. Goce, "Population Pressure and Migration: Implications for Upland Development in the Philippines", *Journal of Philippine Development*, Vol. 15, 1988, pp. 15-46.

268. W. P. David, *Erosion and Sediment Transport* (Philippine Institute for Development Studies, University of the Philippines, Los Banos, Philippines, 1986).

269. W. P. David, *Soil Erosion and Soil Conservation Planning – Issues and Implications* (College of Engineering and Agro-Industrial Technology, University of the Philippines, Los Banos, Philippines, 1987).

270. B. T. Leong and C. B. Serna, *Status of Watersheds in the Philippines* (National Irrigation Administration, Quezon City, Philippines, 1987).

271. Conservation of Fisheries and Aquatic Resources Task Force, *Issues, Problems, and Recommendations in Management and Conservation of Fisheries and Aquatic Resources* (Department of Environment and Natural Resources, Manila, Philippines, 1987).

272. G. T. Silvestre, *Philippine Marine Capture Fisheries – Exploitation, Potential and Options for Sustainable Development* (College of Fisheries, University of the Philippines, Visayas, Diliman, Philippines, 1987); see also G. T. Silvestre and S. Ganaden, *Status of Philippine Demersal Stocks: An Overview* (College of Fisheries, University of the Philippines, Visayas, Diliman, Philippines, 1987).

273. Independent Commission on International Humanitarian Issues, *Famine: A Man-Made Disaster* (Pan Books, London, 1985).

274. B. T. Chidzero, "Africa and the World Economy", *World Futures*, Vol. 25, pp. 157-162, 1988.

275. P. DeCuellar, *Africa's Economic Situation* (Office of the Secretary General, United Nations, New York, 1988).

276. World Bank, *The Challenge of Hunger in Africa: A Call to Action* (The World Bank, Washington DC, 1988).

277. M. M. Dow, "Food and Security", *Bulletin of the Atomic Scientists*, Vol. 41, pp. 21-26, 1985.

278. United Nations World Food Council, *The Global State of Hunger and Malnutrition: 1988 Report* (United Nations World Food Council, New York, 1988).

279. World Hunger Program, *Beyond Hunger: An African Vision of the 21st Century* (World Hunger Program, Brown University, Rhode Island, 1989).

280. L. R. Brown and E. C. Wolf, *Reversing Africa's Decline* (Worldwatch Institute, Washington DC, 1985).

281. T. J. Goliber, *Africa's Expanding Population: Old Problems, New Policies* (Population Reference Bureau, Washington DC, 1989).

282. J. A. Marcum, "Africa: A Continent Adrift", *Foreign Affairs*, Vol. 68, pp. 159-179, 1989.

283. F. T. Sai, "Population Factor in Africa's Development Dilemma", *Science*, Vol. 226, pp. 801-805, 1984.

284. World Bank, *Toward Sustainable Development in Sub-Saharan Africa: A Joint Program of Action* (The World Bank, Washington DC, 1984).

285. G. Farmer and T. M. L. Wigley, *Climatic Trends for Tropical Africa* (Climate Research Unit, University of East Anglia, Norwich, UK, 1985).

286. M. H. Glantz, ed., *Drought and Hunger in Africa* (Cambridge University Press,

Cambridge, UK, 1987).

287. R. S. McNamara, *The Challenges for Sub-Saharan Africa* (Sir John Crawford Memorial Lecture, Washington DC, 1 November, 1985).

288. H. Hurni, *Towards Sustainable Development in Ethiopia* (Institute of Geography, Berne University, Berne, Switzerland, 1990).

289. T. J. Farer, *War Clouds on the Horn of Africa* (Carnegie Endowment for International Peace, Washington DC, 1979).

290. J. Shepherd, *The Politics of Starvation* (Carnegie Endowment for International Peace, Washington DC, 1975).

291. G. Tareke, *Rural Protest in Ethiopia 1961-1970: A Study of Rebellion* (unpublished doctoral dissertation, Syracuse University, Syracuse, New York, 1977).

292. J. Clarke, *Resettlement and Rehabilitation: Ethiopia's Campaign Against Famine* (Gollancz, London, UK, 1986).

293. J. W. Clay and B. K. Holcomb, *Politics and the Ethiopian Famine 1984-85* (Prentice Hall Publishers, Engelwood Cliffs NJ, 1986).

294. C. Eshetu and M. Teshome, *Land Settlement in Ethiopia: A Review of Developments* (Addis Ababa University Press, Addis Ababa, Ethiopia,1984).

295. G. Hancock, *Ethiopia: The Challenge of Hunger* (Gollancz, London, UK, 1985).

296. K. Janson, M. Harris and A. Penrose, *The Ethiopian Famine* (Humanities Press International, Atlantic Highlands NJ, 1987).

297. S. P. Petrides, *The Boundary Question Between Ethiopia and Somalia* (New Social Press, New Delhi, India, 1983).

298. W. B. Selassie, *Conflict and Intervention in the Horn of Africa* (Monthly Review Press, New York, 1980).

299. R. Luckham and D. Bekele, "Foreign Powers and Militarism in the Horn of Africa", *Review of African Political Economy*, Vol. 30, pp. 8-20, 1984; and Vol. 31, pp. 7-28, 1984.

300. D. Gamachu, *Environment and Development in Ethiopia* (International Institute for Relief and Development, Geneva, Switzerland, 1988).

301. G. Kumar, *Ethiopian Famines 1973-1985: A Case Study* (WIDER of the United Nations University, Helsinki, Finland, 1987).

302. K. Tato and H. Hurni, eds., *Soil Conservation for Survival* (Institute of Geography, Berne University, Berne, Switzerland, 1991).

303. D. Gaschen, *Ressourcen-Modell der Regionen Aethiopiens fur die Nachsten 50 Jahre* (Institute of Geography, Berne University, Berne, Switzerland, 1990).

304. A. H. Ehrlich, "Critical Masses", *The Humanist*, Vol. 45, 1985, pp. 18-22.

305. US Department of Agriculture, *World Indices of Agricultural and Food Production 1976-85* (US Department of Agriculture, Washington DC, 1986).

306. C. Juma and R. Munro, *Environmental Profile: Kenya* (Danish International Development Agency, Nairobi, Kenya, 1989).

307. L. O. Odhiambo and J. E. O. Odada, eds., *Kenya's Industrial and Agricultural Strategies: Towards the Year 2000* (United Nations Environment Programme, Nairobi, Kenya, 1988).

308. J. Greer and E. Thorbecke, *Food Poverty and Consumption Patterns in Kenya* (International Labour Organization, Geneva, Switzerland, 1986).

309. M. M. Shah and G. Fischer, *Assessment of Food Production Potential: Resources, Technology and Environment – A Case Study of Kenya* (International Institute for Applied Systems Analysis, Laxenburg, Austria, 1981).

310. C. G. Wenner, "Soil Conservation in Kenya", *Ambio*, Vol. 12, 1983, pp. 305-307.

311. D. W. Brokensha, B. W. Riley and A. P. Castro, *Fuelwood Use in Rural Kenya: Impacts on Deforestation* (Institute for Development Anthropology, State University of New York, Binghampton NY, 1985). ·

312. E. L. Hyman, "The Strategy of Production and Distribution of Improved Charcoal Stoves in Kenya", *World Development*, Vol. 15, 1987, pp. 375-386.

313. P. O'Keefe and P. Raskin, "Crisis and Opportunity: Fuelwood in Kenya", *Ambio*, Vol. 14, 1985, pp. 220-224.

314. Government of Kenya, *Economic Management of Renewed Growth* (Government

Printer, Nairobi, Kenya, 1986).

315. Government of Kenya, *Economic Survey* (Government Printer, Nairobi, Kenya, 1989).

316. A. Kiriro and C. Juma, eds., *Gaining Ground: Institutional Innovations in Land-Use Management in Kenya* (ACTS Press, African Centre for Technology Studies, Nairobi, Kenya, 1989).

317. Kenya National Council for Population and Development, *Kenya Demographic and Health Survey* (Kenya National Council for Population and Development, Nairobi, Kenya, 1989).

318. F. Alba and J. E. Potter, "Population and Development in Mexico Since 1940: An Interpretation", *Population and Development Review*, Vol. 12, 1986, pp. 47-75.

319. R. Godau, "La Proteccion Andrental y la Articulacion Sociedad y Naturaleza", *Estudios Socialogicos*, Vol. 3, 1985, pp. 47-84.

320. I. Restrepo, "Mexico's Environmental Crisis", *Earthwatch* (publication of the International Planned Parenthood Federation, Vol. 18, 1984, pp. 1-7).

321. I. Restrepo, *El Estado del Medio Ambiente en Mexico: Una Vision de Conjunto* (Centro de Escodesarrollo, Mexico City, Mexico, 1986).

322. A. Sherbinin, "Survey Report: Mexico", *Population Today*, Vol. 18, 1990, p. 5 (Earthscan Publications, London).

323. D. M. Liverman, "Drought in Mexico: Climate, Agriculture, Technology and Land Tenure in Sonora and Puebla", *Annals of the Association of American Geographers*, Vol. 80, 1990, pp. 49-72.

324. S. Sanderson, *The Transformation of Mexican Agriculture: International Structure and the Politics of Rural Change* (Princeton University Press, Princeton NJ, 1986).

325. P. L. Yates, *Mexico's Agricultural Dilemma* (University of Arizona Press, Tucson AZ, 1981).

326. L. A. Sancholuz, *Land Degradation in Mexican Maize Fields* (Ph.D. dissertation, University of British Columbia, Vancouver, Canada, 1984).

327. G. Schramm, *The Economics of Soil Conservation in a Semi-Arid Country: Mexico* (School of Natural Resources, University of Michigan, Ann Arbor MI, 1982).

328. R. G. Cummings, *Improving Water Management in Mexico's Irrigated Agricultural Sector* (World Resources Institute, Washington DC, 1989).

329. M. Redclift, "Agriculture and the Environment: The Mexican Experience", in G. Philip, ed., *The Mexican Economy* (Croom Helm, London, UK, 1988).

330. M. S. Grindle, *Official Interpretations of Rural Underdevelopment: Mexico in the 1970s* (Program in US-Mexican Studies, University of California at San Diego, La Jolla CA, 1981).

331. J. L. Posner and M. F. McPherson, "Agriculture on the Steep Slopes of Tropical America: The Current Situation and Prospects", *World Development*, Vol. 10, 1982, pp. 341-353.

332. G. D. Thompson and P. L. Martin, *The Potential Effects of Labor-Intensive Agriculture in Mexico on United States-Mexico Migration* (Commission for the Study of International Migration and Cooperative Economic Development, US Congress, Washington DC, 1989).

333. M. L. Carlos, *State Policies, State Penetration and Ecology: A Comparative Analysis of Uneven Development and Underdevelopment in Mexico's Micro-Agrarian Regions* (Center for US-Mexican Studies, University of California at San Diego, La Jolla CA, 1981).

334. S. Whiteford and L. Montgomery, "The Political Economy of Rural Transformation: The Mexican Case", in B. R. DeWalt and P. J. Pelto, eds., *Micro and Macro Levels of Analysis in Anthropology: Issues in Theory and Research* (Westview Press, Boulder CO, 1984).

335. W. A. Cornelius, *The Cactus Curtain: Mexican Immigration and U.S. Responses* (University of California Press, Berkeley CA, 1991).

336. S. Diaz-Briquets and J. J. Macisco, "Population Growth and Emigration in Latin America: What is the Nature of the Problem?" in J. Saunders, ed., *Population Growth in Latin America and U.S. National Security* (Allen and Unwin, Boston MA, 1986), pp. 79-96.

337. S. Diaz-Briquets, *Conflict in Central America: The Demographic Dimension* (Population Reference Bureau, Washington DC, 1986).
338. A. Schumacher, "Agricultural Development and Rural Employment: A Mexican Dilemma", *Working Papers in U.S.-Mexican Studies No. 21* (Program in United States-Mexican Studies, University of California at San Diego, La Jolla CA, 1981).
339. R. L. Bach and A. Portes, *Latin Journey: Cuban and Mexican Immigrants in the United States* (University of California Press, Berkeley CA, 1985).
340. H. E. Cross and J. A. Sandos, *Across the Border: Rural Development in Mexico and Recent Migration to the United States* (Institute of Governmental Studies, University of California, Berkeley CA, 1981).
341. M. Gendell, "Population Growth and Labor Absorption in Latin America, 1970-2000", in J. Saunders, ed., *Population Growth in Latin America and U.S. National Security* (Allen and Unwin, Boston MA, 1986), pp. 49-78.
342. J. G. Castañeda, "Mexico at the Brink", *Foreign Affairs*, Vol. 64, 1985, pp. 287-303.
343. S. Trejo-Reyes, "Mexico's Long Travail", *Development Forum*, Vol. 15, 1987, p. 10.
344. T. Espenshade, *The Cost of Job Creation in the Caribbean* (The Urban Institute, Washington DC, 1987).
345. United Nations Population Fund, *Population Policies and Programmes in the Latin America and Caribbean Region* (UNFPA Document No. A/E/BD/3 Reg. 4, New York, 1989).
346. J. W. Mellor, "Global Food Balances and Food Security", *World Development*, Vol. 16, 1988, pp. 997-1011.
347. D. Paarlberg, P. M. Cody and R. J. Ivey, *Agrarian Reform in El Salvador* (Checci and Company, Washington DC, 1986).
348. World Bank, *World Development Report 1989* (The World Bank, Washington DC, 1989).
349. W. Durham, *Scarcity and Survival in Central America* (Stanford University Press, Stanford, California, 1979).
350. L. S. Peterson, *Central American Refugee Flows 1978-83* (US Bureau of the Census, Washington DC, 1984).
351. Food and Agriculture Organization of the United Nations, *Land, Food and Population* (FAO, Rome, 1983).
352. United Nations, *World Population Policies, Vols. I and II* (United Nations, Document No. ST/ESA/SER.A/102, New York, 1987).
353. United Nations, *World Fertility Survey – Major Findings and Implications* (WFS, International Statistical Institute, Vaarburg, Netherlands, 1984).
354. W. C. Thiesenhusen, ed., *Searching for Agrarian Reform in Latin America* (Unwin Hyman, Boston MA, 1989).
355. E. B. Barbier, *Sustainable Development, Economics and Environment in the Third World* (Edward Elgar Publishers, Aldershot, UK, 1989).
356. J. Cole, *Development and Underdevelopment: A Profile of the Third World* (Methuen, New York, 1987).
357. P. Demeny, "Demography and the Limits to Growth", *Population and Development Review*, Vol. 14, 1988, pp. 213-244.
358. P. Demeny, *World Population Growth and Prospects* (The Population Council, New York, 1989).
359. M. R. Rosenzweig, "Human Capital, Population Growth, and Economic Development: Beyond Co-relations", *Journal of Policy Modelling*, Vol. 10, 1988, pp. 83-111.
360. World Bank, *World Development Report 1984* (The World Bank, Washington DC, 1984). Note: This edition contains a special section on population change and development.
361. D. Pimentel, L. M. Fredrickson, D. B. Johnson, J. H. McShane and H-W Yuar "Environment and Population: Crises and Policies", in D. Pimentel and C. W. H- eds., *Food and Natural Resources* (Academic Press, New York, 1989).

SOURCES FOR DIAGRAMS, TABLES AND MAP

Table p. 9: adapted from *United Nations World Population Prospects 1990* (United Nations, New York, 1991).

Diagrams p. 10: calculations made on the basis of data provided by United Nations Population Division and N. Sadik, *The State of World Population 1990* (United Nations Population Fund, New York, 1990).

Diagram p. 14: T. W. Merrick, "World Population in Transition", *Population Bulletin*, Vol. 42, No. 2, 1986.

Diagram p. 16: adapted from figures provided by United Nations Population Division.

Diagram p. 17: *Population Pressure and Natural Resource Management: An Assessment of Key Issues and Possible Actions by the ADB* (February 1990).

Table p. 40: M. Falkenmark, "The Massive Water Scarcity Now Threatening Africa - Why Isn't it Being Addressed?", *Ambio*, Vol. 18, 1989, pp. 112-118.

Table p. 46: World Bank, 1989.

Table p. 48: Food and Agriculture Organization of the United Nations, *Fuelwood Supplies in Developing Countries* (1983).

Map p. 50: Food and Agriculture Organization of the United Nations, *Tropical Rainforests: A Disappearing Treasure* (Smithsonian Institution); Norman Myers.

Table p. 54: World Commission on Environment and Development, 1987.

Diagram p. 58: United Nations, 1987, adjusted as per latest available data from 1990 estimates of United Nations.

Table p. 60: United Nations, 1987.

Table p. 92: Myers, 1989.